The
Winning Team

A Guidebook for Junior Showmanship

by Gaile Haynes

Panache Publishing
3041 Glacierwood Drive
Juneau, AK 99801-7137

Elmer E. Rasmuson Library Cataloging-in-Publication Data
Haynes, Gaile.
The winning team : a guidebook for junior showmanship / by Gaile Haynes. [Juneau, Alaska : Panache], c2004.
 p. cm.
1. Dog shows—Junior showmanship classes—Handbooks,manuals, etc.—Juvenile literature. 2. Dogs-Showing—Juvenile literature. I. Title.

SF425.13.H39 2004

Printed in Canada

Design and layout by Sue Mitchell, Inkworks

This book is dedicated to all the juniors over all the years who have made my memories—more than I could ever name, but all of whom I remember in love. And it is for all the dogs who shared with them and with me the joy of showing.

Special thanks to Linda Hollinbeck for use of her camera and for assisting with the cover design, to Karen Parr for providing a Fairbanks base of operations, and to George Haynes, Robert Haynes, Mary Miller, Whitney Sutton, and Mary Thomas who patiently took the photographs; the Alaska Kennel Club members who searched their files for the older pictures; and to Jim Campbell, Jo and Melissa Dahl, Penny King, Mary Miller, Ellen Mitchell, and Karyn Price for editorial help. Sue and Russ Mitchell did a splendid job designing and laying out the final book and drawing the patterns.

I could not have done this without the friendly cooperation of the Alaska Kennel Club, Campbell River Dog Fanciers Society, Glacier View Dog Fanciers Society, Hurricane Ridge Kennel Club, Victoria City Dog Fanciers Society, Yukon Kennel Club, and Western Dog Shows, Ltd.

Taran Haynes and Copper.

Contents

Introduction

The purpose of this book is to introduce new junior handlers, and their parents, to junior showmanship competition—what it consists of, what skills are needed, and where and how to acquire those skills. Although this book will describe and explain each move, nothing takes the place of practice with and without the dog.

For more than twenty-five years I have taught junior showmanship in 4-H classes to several hundred juniors, including my own six children, under both American and Canadian Kennel Club rules.

For some juniors, handling is their major sport. Others, for whatever reason, consider handling as a sometime thing—they enter when it is convenient for them and their parents. Because many factors come into play in determining the amount of the junior's involvement, juniors who show infrequently are not necessarily less interested or less competent than the juniors who spend several weekends every month at dog shows.

But do not think that all juniors come from dog-showing background. Many of the best and most dedicated are the only ones in their family to be involved in the sport.

This book explains the rules for both American and Canadian Kennel Club competition and the difference in philosophy these rules represent. Although 4-H junior showmanship varies considerably from one area to another, I will touch briefly upon it. Even the name of the sport is different in different venues: the Canadian Kennel Club calls it junior

Kathy Steele—now veterinarian Kathy Hawkins—as a young teen showed my Bedlington Terrier, Libby, in a Bedlington specialty show. Although she was the only person in her family to be involved in dog showing, Kathy won several Best Junior Handler awards as well as perfect 200 obedience scores with her Cocker Spaniel Peggy.

handling, while the American Kennel Club calls it junior showmanship. For consistency, and with apologies to the Canadians, I will use the title junior showmanship, but to even things out, refer to the young people as junior handlers or simply juniors.

In this book I write from the viewpoint of teaching my grandson, eleven-year-old Taran Haynes, as he learns to show my Italian greyhound Copper, formally titled Am/Can Ch. Ciel's Toujour la Vie. Taran is a beginning handler, and in real life he does not do all the things that he is supposed to do at every show. These, however, are the skills that he is learning and practicing.

Rules and procedures are complex and technical, and a young junior may need help in reading and interpreting them.

For information on showing or grooming individual breeds and on where to go for information about shows, training, or matches, talk to someone at your local kennel club or your breeder or other doggy affiliate.

STOP HERE. Before going any further, skim in Appendix 1 or 2 the rules for junior showmanship for the American or Canadian Kennel Club, whichever you plan to attend, to get an idea of the intent of junior showmanship and the standards under which it is judged. This book will explain and discuss these rules, and other handling practices.

Where rules or practices differ between the American Kennel Club and the Canadian Kennel Club and 4-H:

American Kennel Club information is boxed like this.

Canadian Kennel Club information is boxed like this.

4-H information is boxed like this.

The Junior Handler

Purpose of Junior Showmanship Competition

The purpose of conformation shows is to select the best breeding stock to create the generations to come. Similarly, the purpose of junior showmanship competition is to help young handlers grow to be a knowledgeable future generation in the sport of showing purebred dogs.

Many of the well-known handlers* of today first started in the junior showmanship rings. Others who never made their mark in the junior showmanship ring are as adults recognized as top handlers. One famous example is Anne Rogers Clark, who describes herself as an awkward teenager who consistently failed to win in junior showmanship competitions. She continued to show her dog in the conformation ring, and as an adult was one of the handling greats of her day until she hung up her leash to become a well-respected international all-breed judge. The skills necessary to become a successful junior are not always the skills that will succeed in handling in the conformation classes.

Where to Learn to Show the Dog

If Taran is to be successful in showing Copper, he must learn how to do it correctly. First, Taran watches the people who handle his breed and other similar breeds. If he can find time when they are not busy, he should talk with them and ask questions. As much as possible—as sexist as this sounds—boys should observe and learn from men, and girls should learn from women, since there are subtle differences in handling style between the sexes.

If there is a 4-H group that teaches junior showmanship, Taran could work with his dog there, always assuming that the leader knows junior handling. Many kennel clubs have handling classes, some especially for juniors. Taran can also study videos of his breed and how to handle it and can read books on his breed and on handling generally.

---

* A handler is the person who shows a dog and may be a professional who receives money for showing someone else's dog.

Only after he has studied proper methods does he begin to practice, because he does not want to practice incorrectly.

In most areas there are matches.* Here Taran can learn to show where the pressure on dog and handler is less intense.

---

* A match is an informal show to train beginning handlers and beginning dogs at which no championship points are earned.

Is Junior Showmanship for You?

What Does Junior Showmanship Offer?

Junior showmanship is perhaps the only sport in which good sportsmanship is not only encouraged but required. Significant failure in this regard can bar a person—junior or adult—from showing.

- Many times in real life people are evaluated on subjective standards. Learning to take this in stride will be of lifetime value to the junior.
- Again in real life, you only get one chance to make a first impression. Juniors learn to make their first impressions count.
- Junior showmanship can help a shy person, since the junior focusing on the dog learns to be less self-conscious.
- A winning junior is likely to move well and to be in good physical condition.
- And finally, junior showmanship puts young people in a sport with their dogs, giving the pleasure of a relationship of mutual love.

Mental Characteristics of the Successful Junior

- A successful junior enjoys competition.
- A successful junior is willing to compete where there are winners and losers.
- A successful junior is comfortable in competition where the judging is subjective. In spite of written standards, the opinion of the judge determines placements.
- A successful junior can shrug off the fact that there are sometimes politics in junior showmanship and unfortunately, the best junior does not always win.
- A successful junior is patient, both in working with the dog and in waiting to achieve success.

Physical Characteristics of the Successful Junior

- The successful junior must have the physical stamina to move the dog at its best gait* for as long as required in all sorts of weather and on all kinds of surfaces.

---

* The gait of the dog is the way it moves. In the show ring, most dogs are moved at a brisk trot.

- The junior must be strong enough to control the dog.

These factors may be compensated for by choosing a dog of a compatible size and temperament for the handler.

- The junior must be able to learn to move smoothly.

Characteristics of the Parents of the Successful Junior

Parents play an important role in their junior's success, whether or not they actively participate.

- They provide the financial support, clothing, and transportation necessary to allow the junior to show.
- They get appropriate training classes, books, and videos for the junior.
- They encourage—but do not nag—the junior to practice.
- They offer emotional support and encouragement.
- They may teach or remind the junior of an instructor's comments.
- They are a pair of eyes to view the junior at practice or in the ring and suggest improvements.

What the parents do not do is also important in their junior's success.

- Parents do not push an unwilling child to participate. Not all young people are interested in this sport in spite of their parents' enthusiasm.
- They do not use junior showmanship as a carrot to secure higher grades or better cooperation around the house.
- They do not encourage the junior to take wins or losses too seriously but do help their child to learn from them.
- They do not rehash mistakes, especially those made in the ring.
- They send their child to get after-action feedback from the judge and do not themselves talk to the judge.

Setting Goals in Junior Showmanship

Many of the difficulties of juniors can be reduced if the junior learns to set realistic goals. There may be only one best junior handler, but for example, Taran as a beginner may set today's goal for himself simply to move Copper smoothly. When he feels confident of his abilities, he can set himself the goal of "making the cut."* Still later, he can set himself the goal of receiving a ribbon in his class. By setting his own goals, he competes at a level in which he feels comfortably challenged.

---

* "Making the cut" means being in the top seven or eight that the judge selects for consideration for the ribbons. Not all judges follow this practice.

The Dog

Where to Get the Dog to Show

Many juniors start with a dog that they or their family already own.

Taran's Aunt Kathy not only showed her own dog but also her brother Robert's Doberman, Alys.

Kathy also had a co-ownership with Donna Coker to show her Basset, Bandit.

In the American Kennel Club juniors may also show dogs that are registered, either fully or with an indefinite listing privilege,* owned or co-owned by members of their immediate family.**

Other juniors are given co-ownerships that allow them to show dogs that do not belong to family members. Some breeders or owners do this simply because they want to encourage juniors, or a particular junior; others may also want to give their semiretired dog a chance to show again and to be seen by others; still others lend dogs to juniors as a way to display the good temperament of their dogs. For example, Taran's Aunt Meg was small as a child. A breeder gave her a large black Great Dane to show. The winning combination of that enormous dog and little girl said more than any words could about the tractability of the dog.

Co-Ownership Contract

When my daughter Kathy showed a Bassett Hound named Bandit, we had a written co-ownership agreement. Even though we were and are on friendly terms with Donna Coker, we both felt it was best to have a simple contract spelling out the terms of co-ownership. Since a minor cannot make a valid contract, as Kathy's parent, I needed to sign the agreement.

Donna added Kathy as co-owner to Bandit's registration certificate and sent the signed certificate to the American Kennel Club. As soon as the papers were returned, Kathy re-signed the registration certificate, but did not date it, listing Donna as sole owner. That way, if anything unexpected happened, Donna only had to send the form back to the American Kennel Club to have full ownership of her dog again.

---

* An indefinite listing privilege is a registration number given by the American Kennel Club to a dog that is apparently purebred but of unknown ancestry, enabling it to be shown in junior showmanship and in performance events, such as obedience and agility. The dog is required to be neutered.

** The "immediate family" is defined by the American Kennel Club as father, mother, brother, sister, uncle, aunt, grandparent, including the corresponding step and half relations, and members of the junior handler's household.

Sample Co-Ownership Agreement

This is an agreement between <u>Donna Coker</u> and <u>Kathy Haynes</u> selling co-ownership of <u>Ch. Margem Hills Bandolero</u> to <u>Kathy Haynes</u> for the purpose of <u>Kathy</u> showing this dog in junior showmanship classes, for the fee of <u>one dollar and other considerations.</u>

   <u>Kathy Haynes</u> may show this dog in junior showmanship classes at <u>Donna Coker's</u> convenience but has no other rights or responsibilities in connection with this dog. <u>Kathy Haynes</u> will pay all junior entry fees. <u>Donna Coker</u> has the sole right to determine in which shows the dog is entered and will pay all conformation entry fees. <u>Donna Coker</u> will retain physical possession of the dog. <u>Kathy Haynes</u> will pay all fees for transfer of ownership. This agreement may be terminated at any time by either party.

Signed <u>*Donna Coker*</u>   Date <u>*Sept. 24, 1973*</u>
Donna Coker

Signed <u>*Kathy Haynes*</u>   Date <u>*Sept. 24, 1973*</u>
Kathy Haynes

Signed <u>*Gaile Haynes*</u>   Date <u>*Sept. 24, 1973*</u>
Gaile Haynes

Back-Up Dog

If Taran gets really serious about showing, he will need to have a back-up dog that he can use if Copper is not available for any reason. A dog that is ill or injured cannot be shown in any class. Bitches* in season cannot be shown in junior showmanship. In those cases, Taran can substitute another eligible dog up to one half-hour before the beginning of the show—that is, one that he or a member of his family owns and that is entered in the show.

In the Canadian Kennel Club Taran enters the day of the show, and, with the owner's permission, may show any dog that is entered in the show that day, whether or not he or his family owns it. Since the dog is entered in the show, it must be registered or listed with the Canadian Kennel Club. Bitches in season may be shown at the discretion of the zone representative in all handling events except for Pee Wee classes. If Taran wants to show a dog that will not be competing in the show for any reason, he enters it "for exhibition only."**

Difference in American and Canadian Philosophy on Ownership

The difference between the American and the Canadian Kennel Clubs' rules represent major differences in philosophy. Although exhibitors must take the rules as they are, it is useful to study the differences and their implications.

The American Kennel Club rules give the advantage to the junior who has trained, or at least seriously worked with, the dog that the junior shows, and they are therefore geared towards producing owner-handlers. The Canadian Kennel Club, by allowing the juniors to handle dogs that are strangers to them, aims at developing professional handlers.

The American Kennel Club limits opportunities for juniors in that if the junior's dog becomes unavailable after entries close, the junior may only substitute another eligible dog, whereas the Canadian junior may select the dog that is most ready on the day of the show.

The American Kennel Club is more likely to have a ring full of serious juniors in that the junior must pre-enter, as opposed to the Canadian Kennel Club, which, by allowing the juniors to enter on the same day, allows impulsive and possibly ill-prepared entrants in the novice classes.

In this litigious society, the American Kennel Club limits the chances of a lawsuit from harm done to a dog or handler attributable to lack of familiarity between the dog and handler.

---

* "Bitch" is the correct term for a female dog. The male is called a dog.

** Dogs entered for exhibition only considered as entrants to the show but are not judged in any class on their own merits.

Before junior showmanship was regulated by the American Kennel Club, it was permitted as a nonregular class. Juniors were allowed to handle dogs other than their own and to enter on the day of the show. I remember groups of juniors canvassing the show area for well-trained and flashy dogs to borrow. This practice created a bad impression of the juniors but does not seem to be in vogue with Canadian juniors.

> In 4-H competition, the dog does not need to be registered, nor even a purebred. The junior showing the dog is expected to have trained and groomed it but does not have to own it. If the dog is a mixed breed, the junior shows it as if it were the breed that it most closely resembles.

Choosing the Right Dog

Just as all young people are not suitable for junior showmanship competition, not all dogs are good choices for the junior ring.

Although it is the junior who is judged and not the dog, Taran would have a difficult time winning with an obviously poor specimen of the breed. A judge is likely to unconsciously expect that the junior with such a dog is not taking handling seriously.

The dog should be well-trained to move and stack* well and should be properly groomed for its breed.

Copper is a natural showman. Taran can succeed more readily with this type of dog than with a dog who is really not interested in being in the show ring and goes grudgingly through his paces with laid-back ears and tail at half-mast.

On the other hand, most judges like to see that the junior has to put forth some effort with the dog, not merely stand there holding the leash while the dog does all the work.

The dog should be of a size and temperament that the junior can handle easily and safely, and of a type that fits the junior physically as well as mentally. A short stocky junior may not be able to gait an Afghan to advantage; a tall lanky junior would overwhelm a Chihuahua.

The Winning Breeds

Are some breeds better than others for junior showmanship? In theory a junior should be able to win with any breed. Certainly in beginning competition this is true. But as the level of competition increases, it is clear that the junior with a flashier breed has an advantage. See the box showing the breeds handled by the winning juniors over the past seventy-plus years at Westminster Kennel Club—one of the most prestigious wins for American juniors.

---

* A stack is the correct show stand for the dog's breed. To stack or set up a dog is to pose it in its correct show stand.

Winning Breeds Handled by Juniors at Westminster

SPORTING

1958	Golden Retriever
1970	Golden Retriever
2001	Golden Retriever
1981	German Shorthaired Pointer
1992	German Wirehaired Pointer
1968	Pointer
2000	Pointer
2003	Pointer
2002	English Setter
1943	Gordon Setter
1959	Irish Setter
1961	Irish Setter
1977	Irish Setter
1994	Cocker Spaniel
1957	Springer Spaniel
1979	English Springer Spaniel
1993	English Springer Spaniel
1998	English Springer Spaniel
1987	Viszla
1985	Weimaraner

HOUND

1956	Afghan
1965	Afghan
1972	Afghan
1991	Afghan
1962	Dachshund
1966	Dachshund
1995	Dachshund
2004	Wirehaired Dachshund
1982	Saluki
1964	Whippet
1971	Whippet

WORKING

1954	Boxer
1963	Boxer
1978	Boxer
1978	Boxer
1999	Boxer
1973	Doberman
1986	Doberman
1989	Doberman
1984	Great Dane
1953	Great Dane
1996	Rottweiler
1997	Siberian Husky
1976	Samoyed

TERRIER

1933	Irish Terrier
1935	Irish Terrier
1955	Irish Terrier
1967	Miniature Schnauzer
1974	Miniature Schnauzer
1960	Scottish Terrier

TOY

(none listed)

NONSPORTING

1948	Boston Terrier
1975	Bulldog
1980	Norwegian Elkhound
1983	Lhasa Apso
1988	Standard Poodle
1990	Standard Poodle

HERDING

1941	Collie
1939	Old English Sheepdog

Some years are missing because in that time period no record was kept of the breed shown. Note that almost all of the winning breeds are medium to large, and none are toys. They are also generally showy, with only two—the Old English Sheepdog and the Bulldog—heavy in movement. Also, they are relatively well-known, rather than new or rare breeds. Although this does not mean that a junior cannot win with dogs outside these categories, the junior will have more difficulty.

Showing in Conformation

It is possible for a junior to win in conformation, even to make group placements, and rarely to win Best in Show. It is not easy in spite of the fact that many juniors show far better than most adult amateur handlers. It is for many reasons easier to finish* a dog using a professional handler than using even a good amateur. These reasons include politics but are more connected with the handler's seriousness in planning a dog's campaign to take advantage of her knowledge of the judges' preferences and prejudices—knowledge gained through years of experience. Not all juniors are free to travel sufficiently to reach the right judge at the right show. Politics and prejudice do enter in. But with patience a title can be won successfully by junior handlers, and there may be no pleasure greater than that of a junior who shows his own dog to his championship.

Taran's Uncle Ben took showing seriously. He showed in obedience, in conformation and in junior showmanship. Here he is finishing his dog Ch. Panache Jingle Bells of D'N'L, C.D., to her championship in regular competition.

---

* To finish a dog is to earn the dog's championship title.

The Dog with a Career

There are several considerations if a junior is showing a dog that has a current show career of his own in the breed ring.

- Although judges must make allowances, there is always the possibility of a scheduling conflict that cannot be resolved.
- Particularly with beginning juniors, some exhibitors fear that the breed judge will see the dog less than perfectly handled by the junior and remember that to the dog's disadvantage in the breed ring.
- Some dogs do not have the stamina to show well in both breed and in heavy junior competition. Especially in hot weather this can be a problem.

On the other hand, for some families, the dog show budget permits no other choice. Awareness of these factors makes it easier to lessen them.

The Judging Schedule

About a week before the show date Taran will receive a judging schedule, which is usually also posted on the Internet. It will show the order in which the dogs are entered and how many dogs are entered in each breed.

Since Taran is showing Copper who is also being campaigned as a breed champion, we study the judging schedule as soon as we receive it to see if there is a possible conflict. If so, we decide before we get to the show which class will be sacrificed. If Taran enters the showmanship ring and then Copper is needed for competition in another ring, Taran excuses himself to the judge, and he may not return to that class.

JUDGING SCHEDULE

RING 1
Mr. Donald M. Booxbaum (103)
9:00 A.M.
1 Greater Swiss Mt Dogs 1-0-0-0
1 Bullmastiffs 0-1-0-0
1 Saint Bernards 0-1-0-0
2 Portuguese Wtr Dogs 1-0-1-0
20 Rottweilers 7-9-3-1

10:00 A.M.
6 Akitas 1-0-2-3
19 Boxers 6-12-1-0
11:00 A.M.
4 Newfoundlands 1-1-2-0
6 Kuvaszok 1-4-0-1
7 Samoyeds 1-4-1-1
13 Siberian Huskies 4-4-2-3

LUNCH

1:00 P.M.
6 Great Pyrenees 4-1-0-1
7 Bernese Mt Dogs 2-2-1-2
10 Doberman Pinschers 6-2-1-1

RING 2
Mr. Eugene Blake (108)
9:00 A.M.
1 Foxhounds (English) 1-0-0-0
2 Weimaraner 1-0-1-0
2 Pointer 0-2-0-0
20 Retrievers (Lab) 7-11-2-0

10:00 A.M.
1 Brittany 0-0-1-0
2 Retrievers (Fc) 2-0-0-0
2 Retreiver (Nsdt) 1-1-0-0
1 Spinone Italiani 0-0-1-0
2 Spaniels (Eng Spr) 0-1-1-0

RING 3
Mr. Edgar L. Bajona (123)
9:00 A.M.
1 Bull Terriers (Clr) 0-1-0-0
1 Soft Coated Whtn Ters 0-0-0-1
1 Parson Russell Terrier 0-0-1-0
3 Fox Terriers (Smooth) 0-1-2-0
3 Cairn Terriers 1-2-0-0
1 Skye Terriers 0-0-1-0
7 Chihuahuas (Sc) 3-2-1-1
5 French Bulldogs 2-1-2-0
3 Shiba Inu 0-1-2-0
10:00 A.M.
10 Chinese Crested 6-4-0-0
12 Chihuahuas (Lc) 2-9-1-0
2 Affenpinschers 0-1-1-0
1 Italian Greyhounds 0-1-0-0

11:00 A.M.
9 Cav King Charles Spans 3-6-0-0
1 Eng Toy Spans (B&pc) 0-0-1-0
1 Havanese 0-1-0-0
5 Papillons 1-3-1-0
1 Lhasa Apsos 1-0-0-0
1 Silky Terriers 0-0-1-0
7 Yorkshire Terriers 2-5-0-0

LUNCH
12:45 P.M.
5 Poodles (Toy) 0-5-0-0
11 Pomeranians 5-4-1-1
5 Poodles (Miniature) 1-4-0-0
5 Schipperkes 1-3-0-1
5 Tibetan Terriers 2-1-2-0
5 Dalmatians 1-3-0-1
4 Keeshonden 0-3-1-0
4 Poodles (Standard) 2-2-0-0
4 Bulldogs 0-2-2-0

continued on next page

8 Setters (Irish) 1-1-2-4
1 Setters (Eng) 0-1-0-0
9 Spaniels (Eng Ckr) 3-4-2-0

11:00 A.M.
1 Spaniels (Ckr) Parti 0-1-0-0
6 Dachshunds (Smooth) 1-3-2-0
1 Beagle 15" 0-0-0-1
9 Dachshunds (Lh) 3-4-1-1
8 Whippets 2-3-2-1
1 Spaniels (Irish Wtr) 0-1-0-0

LUNCH

12:45 P.M.
1 Wirehaired Pt Grfn 1-0-0-0
21 Retrievers (Golden) 6-11-3-1
1 Afghan Hounds 0-0-1-0
3 Borzoi 2-0-0-1
1 Irish Wolfhounds 0-1-0-0
1 Otterhounds 1-0-0-0
1 Rhodesian Ridgebacks 0-0-0-1
2 Basset Hound 1-0-1-0

RING 4
Dr. Sam Burke, Jr. (125)
9:00 A.M.
13 Great Danes 7-3-2-1
4 Belgian Sheepdogs 3-0-0-1
13 Welsh Corgis (Pemb) 5-5-3-0

10:15 A.M.
11 Aust Cattle Dogs 5-4-1-1
3 Welsh Corgis (Card) 0-2-1-0
1 Collies (Rough) 0-0-1-0
2 Belgian Tervuren 0-2-0-0
8 Bouvier Des Flandres 2-4-1-1

11:15 A.M.
1 Polish Lowland Sheepdog 1-0-0-0
16 Australian Shepherds 7-6-1-2
1 Canaan Dogs 0-0-1-0

LUNCH

RING 4
C. Michael Benson (23)
12:00 P.M.
8 Novice Junior
J7, J8, J9, J11, J13, J14, J16, J17,
2 Novice Senior
J20, J21
4 Open Junior
J15, J18, J25, J27
9 Open Senior
J5, J6, J10, J12, J19, J23, J24, J26, J28

RING 4
Dr. Sam Burke, Jr.
1:00 P.M.
26 Shetland Sheepdogs 14-9-2-1
26 German Shepherd Dogs 12-11-2-1

This is a program for a small show, but all programs are similar. The number to the right of the judge's name tells the number of dogs entered under that judge that day. The number to the left of the breed tells how many of that breed are entered. The numbers to the right of the breed break this number down to, in order, the number of class (nonchampion) dogs, the number of class bitches, the number of champion (special) dogs, and the number of champion bitches. Judges are scheduled to judge 25 dogs per hour. They may run late, but they may not start judging before the scheduled time.

The Siberian Huskies in Ring 1 may not be done until 12:15, so a novice junior with a Siberian Husky might have a conflict between the breed ring and the junior handling ring, especially if the breed judge is running late. As soon as the problem becomes apparent, the junior should report it to the ring steward and ask permission to enter the class late if it is necessary. Since we expect that the juniors will not be done until 1 p.m., there will be conflicts for both open senior and best junior handler with breeds that show at 12:45. It is also possible to ask the judge in the breed ring to change the order of the judging, and if no one else is affected, the judge will usually do so. For example, if the single Wire-Haired Pointing Griffon who is supposed to go first in Ring 2 at 12:45 is being handled in junior showmanship, the judge can move its judging until after the Golden Retrievers with no problem for anyone. Since there are five toy Poodles in Ring 3 at 12:45, the judge would probably not be able to move them to another time.

4

Entering a Show

Age Requirements

Juniors who show in both American and Canadian Kennel Club shows should note carefully that the age of eligibility for junior and senior levels not only is actually different but is computed differently.

In American Kennel Club shows, as of January 1, 2005, Taran needs to be at least nine years old on the day of the show to be eligible to compete. As a beginner, he competes in Novice class—Junior for ages 9 through 11 on the date of the show, Intermediate for ages 12 through 14, and Senior for ages 15 through 18. (Some specialty* shows also have Pee Wee classes similar to those in Canada, but those are nonregular and the show-giving clubs can make their own rules.)

After he wins three first-place awards with competition** Taran will graduate to the Open class. He can move on to Open at the same show in which he wins his third Novice win, and he can also upgrade his class in a later show whose entries have already closed. When he advances to another age level, he stays at the level—Novice or Open—that he was in the previous age group. He is not eligible for to compete in Junior Showmanship if he receives payment for handling someone else's dog.

In Canadian Kennel Club shows, as of January 1, 2005, there are two competitive age groups: Novice classes are for junior handlers who have won fewer than six firsts with competition in this class. Junior Novice is for ages 7 through 11 as of December 31 of the competition year.[†] Senior Novice is for ages 12 years and up to but not including 18 years of age as of December 31 of the competition year.

---

* A specialty show is a show for one breed or group of dogs.

** What is meant by "with competition" is with competition in the class. For example, if Taran is the only person in the Junior Novice class but goes on to win Best Junior Handler at that show, the win will not qualify to advance him, as he had no competition in the class.

[†] "Competition year" is the calendar year in which the show is given. For example, Taran turned 11 years of age in July of 2004. In Canadian Kennel Club competition, he was considered to be 11 from January 1, 2004, to December 31, 2004.

(It has been proposed to change the age groups to Pee Wee, 4 through 6 years old; Novice, 7 to through 10 years old; Intermediate, 11 through 14 years old; and Senior, 15 through 17 years old. Another proposed change would make the junior's age computed at the time of the show. I do not know if these proposals will be adopted, but the earliest date they would take effect is January 1, 2006.)

In Canadian Kennel Club shows, when the juniors win six first places, they must move from Novice class to the Open class that corresponds to their age level. Juniors who were in the Junior Open class and who are 12 and over may compete in Senior Novice or go directly to Senior Open. Handlers who have been paid for showing a dog for another person also show in the Senior Open Class.

In addition, the Pee Wee class is for junior handlers 4 through 6 years of age as of December 31 of the competition year. It is optional for the show-giving club and noncompetitive: that is, no placements are made and all entrants receive participant ribbons or rosettes.

In 4-H the lower age limit is first and second grade for Cloverbuds. The individual 4-H region determines whether they may compete in handling. The upper age limit is 19 or completion of 12th grade, whichever comes first. The amount of competition in the region determines the divisions of the classes.

Handler Identification Number

In order to keep track of their wins, junior handlers may receive identification numbers from the appropriate kennel club.

To enter an American Kennel Club show Taran needs a competition number before he can show. To get this number he calls, e-mails, or writes the American Kennel Club, giving his date of birth. He does not have to be a resident of the United States to get this number.

After they enter their first CKC handling competition, junior handlers who are Canadian residents receive an identification number from the Canadian Kennel Club. Residents of other countries do not receive nor need a number to show in Canadian Kennel Club events.

No competition numbers are required in 4-H, but handlers must be 4-H members.

Difference in Philosophy between Canadian and American Kennel Clubs in Entry Numbers

Using the identification numbers to keep track of the juniors' wins, the Canadian Kennel Club yearly selects the best junior handlers from each province or zone. These handlers compete in zonal and final competition, and the best Canadian junior handler of the year is chosen. This competition is described in detail in Chapter 11.

There is no such competition in the United States. Juniors who compete in the limited entry* or invitational competitions,** such as Westminster or Eukanuba, do not compete as representatives of a particular state or region.

Making the Entry

Either Taran or the owner of the dog will complete an entry form, either on paper or online, and send it with the entry fees to the show-giving club or to the show superintendent managing the show, as directed.

> In American Kennel Club shows, the junior showmanship entry is made on the same form and at the same time as the entry in all other classes.

> In Canadian Kennel Club Shows, the junior handling entry is made on the day of the show, usually about an hour before the class is judged. A separate form is used.

The Entry Form

The form must reach its proper destination by the closing date of the show, and there are no exceptions. Some shows with limited entries will reach the assigned number and thus close their entries even earlier.

Be sure to type or print entries clearly and to check all registration numbers and birthdates carefully. At the least, a mistake that keeps the kennel club from recording the win correctly can cost time to straighten out, and it could cost the win itself.

---

* Shows with limited entries are shows that accept only a preset number of dogs due to space or time considerations.

** Invitational shows are those where entry is by invitation only, based on wins in the twelve months previous to the show.

American Kennel Club Form (Front)

OFFICIAL AMERICAN KENNEL CLUB ENTRY FORM
ALL BREED DOG SHOWS AND OBEDIENCE TRIALS
KENAI KENNEL CLUB
☑ **FRIDAY, JULY 9, 2004** ☑ **SATURDAY, JULY 10, 2004** ☑ **SUNDAY, JULY 11, 2004**
Skyview High School - Mile 98 Sterling Highway - Soldotna, Alaska 99669
Entry Fees: - see Page 3
Entries close Wednesday Noon, June 23, 2004 at the Superintendent's office.. MAIL ENTRIES with Fees Payable to **KEVIN ROGERS, P.O. BOX 230, HATTIESBURG, MS 39403-0230**
NOTICE: Please put breed & name of show on checks. I ENCLOSE $ _75.00_ for my entry fees.
IMPORTANT: Read Carefully Instructions on Reverse Side Before Filling Out.
(PLEASE PRINT)

BREED Italian Greyhound	VARIETY (1)	SEX male

DOG (2) (3) SHOW CLASS specials only	CLASS (3) DIVISION Weight, Color, Etc.

ADDITIONAL CLASSES	OBEDIENCE TRIAL CLASS	JR. SHOWMANSHIP CLASS

NAME OF (See Back) JUNIOR HANDLER Taran Haynes	JR. HANDLER AKC # 19930721001

FULL NAME OF DOG Ch. Ciel's Toujour la Vie

☑ AKC REG. NO ☐ AKC LITTER NO. ☐ ILP NO. ☐ FOREIGN REG. NO. & COUNTRY	Enter number here TR061413/01	DATE OF BIRTH 6/13/2002
		PLACE OF BIRTH ☑USA ☐CANADA ☐FOREIGN DO NOT PRINT THE ABOVE IN CATALOG

BREEDER Cemela Dee London

SIRE Ch. L'Images One Destiny of Retaggio

DAM Ch. Ciel Rohan's Zazzle Dazzle

ACTUAL OWNER (S) (4) Gaile Haynes

OWNERS ADDRESS PO Box 12345   (Please Print)

CITY Juneau   **STATE** AK   **ZIP + 4** 99801

NAME OF OWNER'S AGENT
(IF ANY) AT THE SHOW   Sandy Smith

I CERTIFY that I am the actual owner of the dog, or that I am the duly authorized agent of the actual owner whose name have entered above. In consideration of the acceptance of this entry, I (we) agree to abide by the rules and regulations of the American Kennel Club in effect at the time of this show or obedience trial, and by any additional rules and regulations appearing in the premium list for this show or obedience trial or both, and further agree to be bound by the "Agreement" printed on the reverse side of this entry form. I (We) certify and represent that the dog entered is not a hazard to persons or other dogs. This entry is submitted for acceptance on the foregoing representation and agreement.

SIGNATURE of owner or his agent
duly authorized to make this entry *Gaile Haynes*

Telephone (907) _123-4567_

E-mail Address: _ghaynes@ak.net_

Credit Card _____ Exp. Date _____
MC☐ Visa ☐ AmEx☐ Disc☐

In American Kennel Club shows, the junior showmanship entry is made on the same form and at the same time as the entry in all other classes.

American Kennel Club Form (Back)

INSTRUCTIONS

1. (Variety) if you are entering a dog of a breed in which there are varieties for show purposes, please designate the particular variety you are entering, i.e., Cocker Spaniel (solid color Black, ASCOB, parti-color), Beagles (not exceeding 13 in. over 13 in. but not exceeding 15 in.) Dachshunds, (long-haired, smooth, wirehaired), Bull Terriers (colored, white), Manchester Terriers (standard, toy), Chihuahuas (smooth coat, long coat), English Toy Spaniels (King Charles and Ruby, Blenheim and Prince Charles), Poodles (toy, miniature, standard), Collies (rough, smooth).

2. The following categories of dogs may be entered and shown in Best of Breed competition; Dogs that are Champions of Record and dogs, which according to their owners records, have completed the requirements for a championships, but whose championships are unconfirmed. The showing of unconfirmed Champions in Best of Breed competition is limited to a period of 90 days from the date of the show where the dog completed the requirements for a championship.

3. (Event Class) Consult the classification in this premium list. If the dog show class in which you are entering your dog is divided, then in addition to designating the class, specify the particular division of the class in which you are entering your dog, i.e., age division, color division, weight division.

4. A dog must be entered in the name of the person who actually owned it at the time entries for a show closed. If a registered dog has been acquired by a new owner, it must be entered in the name of its new owner in any show for which entries closed after the date of acquirement, regardless of whether the new owner has received the registration certificate indicating that the dog is recorded in his name. State on entry form whether transfer application has been mailed to A.K.C. (For complete rule refer to Chapter 11, Section 3).

If this entry is for Jr. Showmanship, please give the following information:

JR'S AKC # 1 9 9 3 0 7 2 1 0 0 1   JR'S DATE OF BIRTH 7/21/93

ADDRESS PO Box 12345

CITY Juneau   STATE AK   ZIP+4 99801

If Jr. Handler is not the owner of the dog identified on the face of this form, what is the relationship of the Jr. Handler to the owner? Grandson

By signing this entry form I/we certify that the Junior Showman does not now, and will not at any time, act as an agent/handler for pay while continuing to compete in Junior Showmanship.

Taran Haynes

Junior's Signature

Note that faxed entries must also have the back faxed, to show it has been read, even if there is no junior showmanship entry.

Canadian Kennel Club Regular Form

OFFICIAL CANADIAN KENNEL CLUB FORM

Skaha Kennel Club

Conformation	Conformation/Obedience	Conformation/Obedience
☑ Fri. Sept. 17, 2004	☑ Sat. Sept. 18, 2004	☑ Sun. Sept. 19, 2004
	Obedience ☐ Tr.# 1 ☐ Tr.# 2	Obedience ☐ Tr.# 1 ☐ Tr.# 2

ENTRIES CLOSE: WEDNESDAY, SEPTEMBER 1, 2004 (12:00 Noon)

Phone (250) 573-3944	All fees payable to and mailed to: Western Dog Shows Ltd., Show Secretary PO Box 3070 M.P.P., Kamloops BC Canada V2C 6B7	Fax (250) 573-3574

Entry Fees $ 66.00 Listing Fees $ _____ Catalogue $ 6.00 P/F Chg $ _____ Total $ _____
(please refer to the premium list for daily charges)

Enter in the following classes:

☐ Junior Puppy ☐ Open
☐ Senior Puppy ☑ Specials Only
☐ Canadian Bred ☐ Exhibition Only
☐ Bred By Exhibitor ☐ Brace Class

Obedience Jumps:
High _____ in.
Broad _____ in.

☐ Novice A ☐ Pre-Novice
☐ Novice B ☐ Novice Intermediate
☐ Open A ☐ Novice C
☐ Open B
☐ Utility
☐ Exhibition Only

Please print or type entry form clearly

Breed __Italian Greyhound__ Variety _____ Sex __male__

Reg'd Name of Dog __Ch. Ciel's Toujour la Vie__

Check One and Enter Number Here
☐ CKC Reg. No.
☑ CKC ERN Number __02144230__
☐ CKC PEN Number
☐ CKC Misc. Cert. No.
☐ Listed (No CKC/ERN/PEN No.)

Date of Birth: M __6__ D __13__ Y __2002__ Is this a Puppy? Yes ☐ No ☑

Place of Birth: Canada ☐ Elsewhere ☑

Breeder(s) __Cemela Dee London__

Sire __Can/Am. Ch. L'Images One Destiny of Retaggio__

Dam __Can/Am. Ch. Ciel Rohan's Zazzle Dazzle__

Reg'd Owner __Gaile Haynes__

Owner's Address __PO Box 12345__

City/Prov/Country __Juneau, Alaska, USA__ P.Code __99801__

Agent (if any) __Michelle Yeadon__

Agent's Address _____

City/Prov/Country _____ P.Code _____

Mail acknowledgements to (check <u>one</u> only): OWNER ☑ or AGENT ☐

I accept full responsibility for all statements made on this entry. I hereby certify that I understand the CKC rules and regulations, conditions and provisions in the Premium List for this show and I agree to be bound by the same.

Credit Card # _____ Expiry Date _____

Name of Cardholder _____
(Please print or type clearly)

Signature of Cardholder _____ ☐ MasterCard ☐ VISA

Signature of Owner/Agent *Gaile Haynes* Ph.# (907) __123-4567__

Email address: __ghaynes@ak.net__

➪ *ALL electronic entries rec'd within 72 HOURS of closing time, will be assessed a processing fee of $3.00 (per day entered)*

Note that there is nowhere to place a junior handling entry on this form.

Canadian Kennel Club Junior Handling Form

JUNIOR HANDLING ENTRY FORM

Instructions
- Form to be typed or printed in ink
- All signatures to be written in ink and not printed
- Please forward all entry forms to CKC when sending in results.

Name of Club: Skaha Kennel Club

Date of Event: Friday Sept. 17, 2004   **Event:** ☑ Conformation   ☐ Obedience

OBEDIENCE	
☐ Junior Novice A	☐ Senior Novice A
☐ Junior Novice B	☐ Senior Novice B
☐ Junior Open A	☐ Senior Open A
☐ Junior Open B	☐ Senior Open B

CONFORMATION	
☐ Pee Wee	
☑ Junior Novice	☐ Senior Novice
☐ Junior Open	☐ Senior Open

Name: Taran Haynes   **Junior Handler No.:**

Address: PO Box 12345

City: Juneau   **Province:** AK, USA   **Postal Code:** 99801

Telephone #: (907) 123-4567   **Birthdate:** July 21, 1993

Breed of dog: Italian Greyhound   **Armband No.:** 137

Taran Haynes
Signature of Junior Handler

Gaile Haynes
Signature of Parent/Guardian

Obedience
Junior Novice A - Open to handlers 7 years of age and up to and including 11 years of age as of December 31st of the competition year who have not earned 300 points in a Junior Obedience Class.

Junior Novice B - Open to handlers 7 years of age, up to and including 11 years of age as of December 31st of the competition year who have earned 300 points.

Junior Open A - Open to handlers 7 years of age, up to and including 11 years of age as of December 31st of the competition year who have not earned 300 points in the Open class. The dog must have its CD title before it may compete in this class.

Junior Open B - Open to handlers 7 years of age, up to and including 11 years of age as of December 31st of the competition year who have earned 300 points in the Open class. The dog must have its CD title before it may compete in this class.

Senior Novice A - Open to handlers 12 years of age, up to but not including 18 years of age as of December 31st of the competition year who have not earned 300 points in a Junior Obedience class.

Senior Novice B - Open to handlers 12 years of age, up to but not including 18 years of age as of December 31st of the competition year who have earned 300 points.

Senior Open A - Open to handlers 12 years of age, up to but not including 18 years of age as of December 31st of the competition year who have not earned 300 points in the Open class. The dog must have its CD title before it may compete in this class.

Senior Open B - Open to handlers 12 years of age, up to but not including 18 years of age as of December 31st of the competition year who have earned 300 points in the Open class. The dog must have its CD title before it may compete in this class.

Conformation
Pee Wee Class - This class is for handlers 4 to 6 years of age as of December 31st of the competition year. This class is optional and non-competitive. No placements are to be awarded; only participant ribbons, rosettes and token trophies may be presented.

Junior Novice Class - This class is for handlers 7 years of age and up to and including 11 years of age as of December 31st of the competition year, who have not won 4 first places in the same class with competition.

Junior Open Class - This class is for handlers 7 years of age and up to and including 11 years of age as of December 31st of the competition year who have won 4 places with competition. It is understood that once the handler has entered and competed in the Junior Open Class, he may not compete in the Junior Novice Class again.

Senior Novice Class - This class is for handlers 12 years of age and up to but not including 18 years of age as of December 31st of the competition year who have not won 4 first places with competition in this class. Handlers from the Junior levels progress to this class.

Senior Open Class - This class is for handlers 12 years of age and up to but not including 18 years of age as of December 31st of the competition year who have won 4 first places with competition, in the Senior Novice Class, and for any handler who has progressed through the Junior Open level and feels that he has enough experience to compete at this level. This class is also for handlers who have received some type of monetary consideration for showing a dog at the Junior or Senior level.

About an hour before the class, the show secretary gives out separate forms to use for Junior Handling.

5

What to Wear?

The Overall Picture

If we consider Copper as a picture that Taran is presenting to the judge, Taran is the frame that sets off the picture. Therefore, Taran should first of all be neat and clean and dressed in colors and styles that look good on him and that best show off the dog.

Basic Necessities

Generally speaking, junior showmanship calls for formal sports clothes. The illustrations used throughout this book show the wide variety of appropriate clothes.

- Pockets are a must. (There are bait* bags that a handler can pin to a dress or slide onto a belt, but they tend to be unattractive.)
- Shoes should be comfortable, with nonskid soles, flat heels, not clunky, and with no chance of slipping off.
- Hair should be neat, off the handler's face, and not in an extreme style.
- Handlers may not wear anything that identifies them as belonging to any group—no Scout neckerchiefs, club blazers, or the like.

Use of color is important. A junior wearing neutral colors for skirt or pants and jacket should wear a bright shirt, tie, or blouse to call attention to the dog. Solid color clothes are generally better to wear when showing parti-colored** dogs, while solid-colored dogs look well against plaids, stripes, or dots. Small juniors and those with small dogs that tend to get lost in the crowd should wear a stand-out color at least as an accent.

Check the elastic in all clothes—including undergarments. I can remember when the elastic broke on mine in the show ring. It was embarrassing.

Also have someone check the clothes to be sure that, no matter what moves you make, they do not show anything better left hidden nor do they reveal anything when you stand against a strong light or move fast or in a heavy breeze.

---

* Bait is the food treat or attention-getting device. See Chapter 10, "Bait and Toys."

** Parti-colored dogs are those of more than one color.

If the show is held outdoors, Taran has raingear that he can wear until he actually goes in the ring. He wears clothes that will stand up to the rain without wilting while he is showing.

Clothes for Boys

Boys wear shirts with ties and jackets or dress sweaters except in very hot weather. Western string ties are acceptable, if they coordinate with the dog and the handler's outfit. At informal outdoor shows boys may wear sports shirts without ties. Ties should be tacked down.

Clothes for Girls

Girls can wear skirts, skorts, or pants suits. Although girls have more choices than boys, they also have more clothing hazards, as it is important to choose a skirt length that does not interfere with nor hide the dog but one that is not too short or tight for bending or kneeling. Avoid scarves, jewelry, ruffles, ribbons, low-cut blouses, and other frou-frou. A good place to shop for the correct style of girls' clothes is in the adult sections of stores.

6

Presenting the Dog

Basic Grooming

Copper is properly groomed according to the breed standard and absolutely clean. His teeth are brushed and his toenails clipped. Copper needs little grooming, but junior handlers with coated* dogs must study the breed standard and then talk to breeders and handlers to learn how to groom their dogs to their best advantage.

Leashes and Collars

Not only must Taran be properly dressed, Copper should also wear the correct leash and collar for the ring. The leash and collar should:

- like every other piece of show gear, be clean and in good condition;
- blend with the coloring of the dog, so that it does not distract from the smooth lines of the dog; and
- be strong enough to control the dog easily.

There are several possible leashes and collars that are suitable for this show ring. Taran talks to handlers of his breed for recommendations.

Large or hard-to-control dogs may be shown on a choke chain and a narrow lead of leather or fabric. The next level of control are martingale lead-collar combinations, while the various types of slip leads give least control. Most toy dogs are shown on extremely narrow leads, but Copper moves too rapidly and so needs a leash/collar that is wide enough that it does not cut into his neck.

Use a smooth lead/collar on a coated dog, so that the coat does not catch in the woven collar. Jeweled choke chains look good on short-coated breeds but should not be used with long-coated dogs since they pinch the coat.

The choice between the leads and collars is otherwise a matter of handler and dog preference and size. Taran always has an extra leash available in case the one he is using breaks. Copper once chewed through his show lead, and since there were none for sale at the show, I had to show him using a bootlace as a leash—carrying an extra lead is better.

---

* A coated dog is one having other than a short coat.

Note that the lead is folded in Taran's hand and will be almost completely hidden when he turns his hand over in the correct position.

Holding the Leash

Taran holds the leash folded like an accordion and completely hidden by his hand, with no part left dangling. It looks neat, and can be played out from his fingers as necessary to give Copper more lead. He holds the leash so that the collar is at the top of Copper's neck, right behind the ears.

Taran's arm is in a relaxed position held straight down from his shoulders. With a small dog, his thumb is up and his fingers face forward. The leash is perpendicular to the ground but noticeably loose. A taller dog may have the leash held more nearly horizontal, but still behind the dog's ears. The hand is held knuckles up. If the dog is of a breed that should be shown with its head up, but it does not do so, use the leash to hold it up, but not so tightly that the dog's front feet barely touch the ground.

Taran demonstrates an incorrect way to hold the lead, wrapped around his hand. He cannot readily let go of the lead when he needs to. But note the rubber band fitting into the notched armband, discussed in the next chapter.

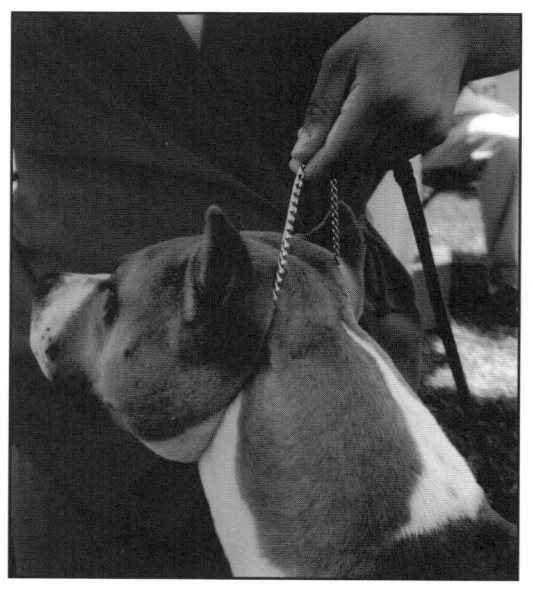

Ashley demonstrates the correct way to place the collar, well up behind the dog's ears. She is using a jeweled choke chain that looks well on her smooth-coated dog and provides good control.

Entering the Ring

Show Grounds Manners

Taran is aware of the need for good manners at all times on the show grounds. He picks up after his dog and himself, of course. He keeps Copper safe from other dogs and does not allow Copper to touch or sniff other dogs. He also offers to help other exhibitors in any way that he can. He goes out of his way to be polite and considerate, because not all adults at a dog show understand, or even like, children.

The Armband

Well before it is time for his class to begin Taran picks up his armband. He will also be given a rubber band to fasten the armband around his left arm. He notches the armband, so that it does not slide down through the rubber band.

In American Kennel Club shows, Taran picks up his armband at the ringside from the ring steward. He should know his armband number from the entry form he received before the date of the show or from the catalog number. It will be a different number from Copper's in the competition ring. He will pick up a new armband for each day of the show.

In Canadian Kennel Club shows, he picks up his armband at the show superintendent's table. Copper will use the same number for any class he is in that day, including juniors. He will use the same armband for the entire show weekend.

Resolving Time Conflicts

Taran also speaks to the ring steward about any time conflicts he may have. The steward does not have the authority to allow him to come late but will relay his problem to the judge. If he is not going to show in this class for any reason, he should tell the steward so that he can be marked absent.

Exercising the Dog

One of the most important things that Taran does is to exercise* Copper before he takes him in the ring. This is important because it is embarrassing at best to have the dog relieve himself in the ring, and Copper will move badly if he is holding himself in to avoid doing so. Both indoor and outdoor shows have areas that can be used for this purpose, and other areas that are forbidden. In all cases, Taran uses the "pooper scoopers" provided for the purpose and carries an emergency plastic bag to pick up poop. Most dogs that travel to shows are taught a command that means "go here," since the exercise area may not have the surface that the dog is accustomed to using.

If, in spite of this, Copper does foul the ring, Taran stands in one spot to let him finish. This is one time that he usually does not clean up after his dog—ordinarily the ring steward will see to it, although Taran should offer to do so.

Taran also visits the restrooms and makes a last minute check of himself in a mirror.

Outside the Ring

When the class forms outside the ring, the steward will line everyone up. Usually for the judge's convenience, the lineup is in order by armband or catalog number. Taran, as much as possible, keeps Copper sheltered between his body and the ring barriers. This will protect Copper from aggressive or poorly controlled dogs as well as from petting by spectators or offers of food from anyone. Although the judging does not begin until the class enters the ring, the judge may nevertheless be watching and Taran may make an irrevocable first impression, good or bad, by what he does at this point.

Getting Psyched Up

At this point, Taran "psychs up" Copper. Some dogs may need play with a toy or a little bait to get them excited enough to show well. Others, especially young dogs, may need to be steadied down.

Here the class is forming outside the ring. The ring steward, wearing the hat, holds the list of entrants and reads out the armband numbers. The class stands in a line in front of her.

---

* "Exercising" the dog is a polite way of saying he gives the dog a chance to relieve himself—a "potty run."

Taran also pyschs himself up. He reminds himself of how good Copper is and how much his handling skills have improved. Nervousness causes adrenaline to flow. To keep himself from breathing its fumes at Copper and making him nervous, Taran sucks a breath mint.

Entering the Ring

When he actually enters the ring, Taran is completely ready. He is holding the leash correctly, and Copper is sparkling with excitement and ready to go. Taran steps out confidently and smoothly when his number is called and makes pleasant eye contact with the judge. He goes around the ring, which ordinarily is square or rectangular, counterclockwise to where the dogs are being set up.* In a large class the first dog may go completely around and end up facing the ring entrance, or line up immediately beyond the ring gate. In a small class with a rectangular ring the judge may line the dogs up on the long side of the ring to get a better overall view of them.

Ashley poses with her American Staffordshire terrier. She has moved too far back and Bert and Sean Johnson with the Norwegian Elkhounds on either side screen her dog from the judge's view. To keep this from happening, she should have moved her dog as close to the center of the ring as the dog in front of her, or she should have stayed where the back Elkhound is now. There is no way that she can correct the situation unless the two Elkhounds can move enough to give her room.

---

* Set up is another term for stack. So, dogs that are set up are standing in show position.

WARNING: The procedures described here and in the following chapters are the usual procedures followed by most judges. If a judge tells Taran to do something different from what is described here, Taran does exactly what the judge tells him as best he can.

Spacing in the Ring

Taran is careful to stay well behind the dog ahead of him—about two giant steps is a good distance. This gives him room to move in case the handler behind him crowds him. He is especially careful not to get crowded into a corner where Copper could be completely blocked from the judge's view.

Once he is in line, Taran stacks Copper and keeps him there, without fussing with him. If the dog behind him crowds him, Taran politely asks the handler to step back. If this does not work, Taran stands or kneels with one foot or knee behind Copper, so that the dog cannot get too close. If Taran has to kneel to show a dog, he kneels on one knee only so that he can get up and move quickly when it is time.

In this posed picture, Bert (right) has been consistently running up too close to the dog in front. To protect his dog, Sean (left) stands with one foot behind his dog so that Bert cannot get too close.

If the show is an indoor show the rings are ordinarily matted, and Taran keeps Copper on the mat at all times unless he is specifically told to do otherwise by the judge. Because Copper is a small dog, Taran stacks him at the edge of the mat nearest the center of the ring so that he is not hidden from view by larger dogs. When there is a table in the ring, Taran never lets the judge's view of Copper be blocked by it.

Proper Gait

At all times when he is moving Copper, Taran moves him at his best speed. Even if Copper moves far more slowly than the dog in front of him, he does not let himself get flustered into changing his own dog's correct gait. If he is behind a slower-moving dog, he holds Copper back when they are behind the judge, and speeds up to the correct gait when they are in the judge's line of sight.

The Dog Behind

If the handler behind him lets his dog run up too close behind Copper, Taran first asks him to be more careful. If the handler continues to do this, through inexperience or bad manners, Taran "accidentally" drops a piece of bait or other equipment in motion. He stops to pick it up, pulling Copper out of the way, lets the other dog pass him, and moves back to the end of the line. It is never proper to pass another dog in the ring unless told to do so by the judge.

Stacking the Dog

When Taran gets to his place in line, he sets up his dog. An easy way for Taran to get the front feet into position is to place his hands on either side of Copper's skull just behind the eyes and lift Copper by the head until his front feet are about an inch off the ground. Taran drops

Taran illustrates the wrong way to correct a front stack. He is holding Copper by the foreleg and trying to persuade Copper to put weight on the foot. Since Copper is un-balanced by this, he only resists harder.

Andrew Owens, with the English Cocker Camai's Mystique Lace, is correcting the dog's front stack. He grasps the dog by the elbow and moves the leg.

him gently with Copper's front feet well under his chest, and, because Copper is well-made in front, the front feet will fall into place. To make a minor correction, Taran can shift Copper's weight by pulling the lead away from the foot that needs to be moved. This will make Copper lift that foot and replace it correctly without Taran apparently moving the dog. If necessary Taran corrects any misplacement, moving the outside* foot first, grasping it at the elbow.

Then Taran places the back legs. He moves the outside back leg first into its correct position, by grasping it at the hock. In the same way he moves the inside back leg. He checks Copper to be sure everything is all right. If he were showing a dog whose tail was held, he would hold it in the correct position for the breed. The tail may be lifted into various angles, depending upon the breed, but it is never clutched. When Copper is stacked, Taran uses a little bait to get his head at the correct angle and his ears alert.

Ashley reaches under her dog to stack the outside leg.

You can just see Adam Smith's hand as he correctly sets the inside rear leg of his German Shepherd, Marydon's Northern Temptation. When he checks, Adam will notice that her front legs are still a little too close together.

---

* The outside foot is the foot nearest the center of the ring. The inside foot is the foot nearest the handler.

Free Stacking

Some breeds are expected to free stack, that is, to come into the correct stand without the handler touching their legs or feet. Dogs of these breeds must be taught to move into the right position by using bait to lure them into position. The handler may also use the leash to slightly shift the dog's weight, causing its foot to move.

Meghan Munter corrects her Doberman's free stack by pulling the leash to the side to shift its weight. At the same time she holds bait to her mouth to keep her dog's attention.

8

Showing the Dog

Usual Ring Procedure

The usual judging procedure is:

- The handlers enter the ring counterclockwise and stack their dogs facing in the direction of the move. At this point the judge usually surveys the class as a whole. Taran makes eye contact with him and may smile politely—a "Good morning, Judge" kind of smile.
- The judge usually arranges the class in order of the speed of the dogs' gait, and may divide the class if it is large.
- The judge views the class (or section of the class) as a whole. Again Taran makes friendly eye contact.
- The judge moves everyone in the class at the same time. He may say, "Take them around," or simply wave a hand in the direction the group is to move. When the judge tells the first person to start, it is ring courtesy for that person to ask the next one in line, "Are you ready?" When the class stops, each handler stacks his dog.
- The judge examines each dog individually and then asks the handler to move it in a pattern to show its gaits from all viewpoints. As soon as the dog ahead of Taran is performing its pattern, Taran gets Copper ready. He puts him on the table, unless the judge tells the handlers not to do this. (The judge might tell the handlers to wait because the judge may want to see how well the handler can put the dog on the table or ramp.)
- The judge may again move the class in unison or may choose the best six or eight handlers before doing this. At the point where the judge is choosing the top handlers Taran looks at the judge cheerfully and proudly. He knows he has done a good job with Copper—or at least worked hard—and he is sending mental messages to the judge, reminding him how good he and Copper were. He may also use his hand subtly to point out Copper's best feature.
- The judge may make a tentative arrangement in order of placing, and then move the group in unison, or the judge may move the group in unison and place the dogs in order as they move. Taran knows that it is important to keep working with his dog until the

final moment where the judge has marked the book and is handing out the ribbons. Sometimes in the last few seconds, the judge will change the placing.

- On the side of the ring by the entrance are numerals that show the order of placing. When the judge chooses the winners, they line up by these numbers and show the judge or ring steward their armband numbers. They thank the judge for the ribbon and congratulate the first-place winner.

The Divided Class

After all the dogs are in the ring, the judge will probably arrange the dogs by size and may divide the class for ease of judging and for safety. There are several ways that this division may be done, depending in part on the size of the ring and the size of the group:

- If the class is large for the size of the ring, the judge may divide the class and send half completely outside the ring.
- If there is room in the ring, the judge may have the half of the group move to the center of the ring and first move the remaining dogs, and then have the groups change places.
- An alternative way to divide is to move part of the group back against the ring barriers.

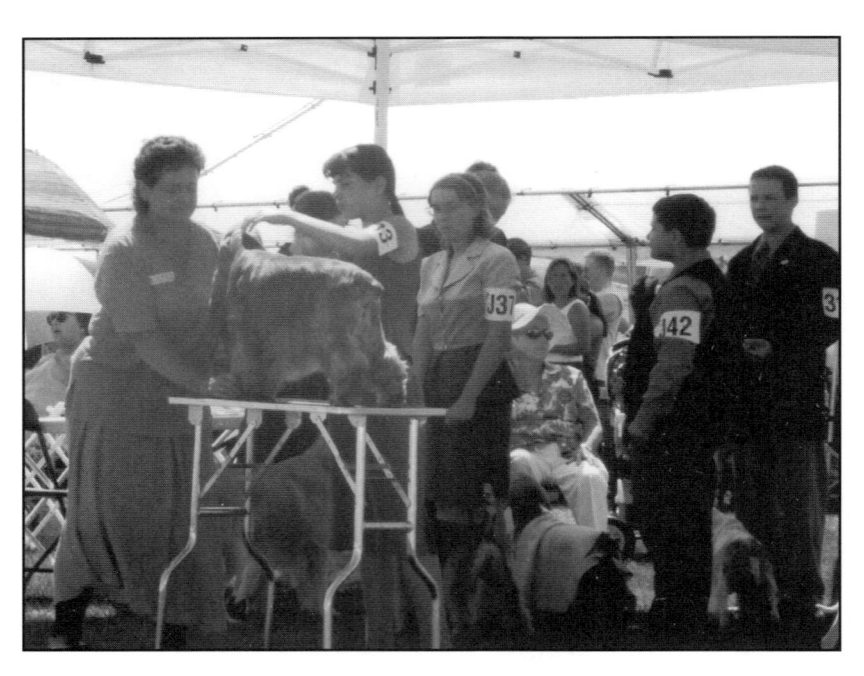

The judge, Dr. Vandra Huber, divided this class and, since it is a hot day, she examines the cocker spaniel on the table under the shade of the tent. Note the cooling blankets on the dogs waiting their turn.

In any type of division the judge may work each part of the class separately and then bring the whole class together to make the placings, or the judge may choose the top four from each division—without giving the order of placing—and then bring back only those top four to make the final division.

Relaxing the Dog in a Divided Class

In the first instance of dividing the class, when Taran is outside the ring he can relax Copper completely, but he must still be immediately
ready to return to the ring and show him.

When the juniors remain in the ring but are not being judged, the judge will usually tell them to relax their dogs. As always, the junior must follow the judge's instructions. On the other hand, the junior should keep the dog alert and ready to be shown as soon as the judge calls for them. How this is done will depend upon the individual dog's temperament. But the handler, when told to relax the dog, should not keep the dog in a show stack unless the dog assumes it naturally.

Relaxing the Dog while Individual Examinations are Done

While the judge is conducting the individual examinations he usually does not tell the handlers to relax their dogs. Therefore, they should not do so. This does not mean that Taran should try to keep Copper in a perfect show stack. It does mean that Copper should be standing evenly and ready to be seen by the judge with just a quick fix by the handler.

Procedure for Individual Examinations

In the individual examination the judge will examine the dog from front to rear, usually starting by standing back to get a good overall view of the dog's expression. This is one of the times when Taran might use a piece of bait or a toy to attract Copper's attention and make him look alert.

Using the Table or Ramp

The purpose of the table or ramp is to raise the dog to a height where the judge can examine it without having to kneel. Small lightweight dogs are stacked on the table. Heavier dogs, such as Bassets and Corgis, are shown on a platform with a ramp leading to it. The ramp raises the dog for the judge to examine without the handler having to lift it. Handlers who use these aids have an extra opportunity to show the judge both that their dogs are well trained and that they are careful for the dogs' safety in mounting and dismounting. (Tables or ramps are not used in Pee Wee classes.)

Since Taran shows a dog from the toy group, he will stack Copper on a table. He lifts Copper carefully and stacks him with his front paws at the front edge of the table. He drapes the leash around his neck and then stacks Copper as described in Chapter 7. (Some handlers recommend holding the leash instead of draping it around the neck, but this is hard for beginning juniors and those with small hands.) When he is finished, he lifts him just as carefully and puts him down gently. He never allows Copper to jump on or off the table.

Taran starts to lift Copper onto the table. Note how his right hand is in front of Copper's chest so that Copper cannot jump forward out of his arms.

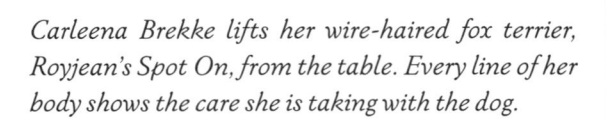

Carleena Brekke lifts her wire-haired fox terrier, Royjean's Spot On, from the table. Every line of her body shows the care she is taking with the dog.

Handlers who use a ramp are careful to lead the dog all the way up and down the ramp, not letting it jump off the sides.

Showing the Bite or Teeth

After the judge has taken an overall view, he will ask Taran to show his dog's bite.* To do this, Taran rests Copper's jaw on his right hand and uses his thumb to pull down the lower lip. At the same time, he gently places his left hand over Copper's nose, and with his thumb and first finger lifts the upper lip. For breeds that require a minimum number of teeth in the dog's mouth, the handler will also be asked to show all the dog's teeth. Those handlers must open their dog's mouth completely so that the judge can count the dog's teeth. Chow Chows and Chinese Shar-Peis must also show their blue tongue. In any case, be sure that the dog is facing the judge with its head at an angle that allows the judge to see the teeth or tongue.

Note how Katlyn McDonald correctly opens the mouth of her German Shepherd, Can/Am Ch. Lindau's Thief of Hearts, to show its bite. Since her hands are large enough, she can pull the lips back far enough to show the side teeth also.

Katlyn opens her dog's mouth wide so the judge can count the teeth. Note how she tilts the head back to make it easy for the judge.

---

* The dog's bite is the way the dog's teeth meet in his mouth—do the top teeth touch the bottom teeth in front of or behind them or not touch them at all?

Judge's Hands-On Examination

Now the judge will examine the dog with his hands, going from front to back. The handler has two jobs to do—keep the dog in position and keep out of the way of the judge.

To accomplish the first, Taran holds the leash straight up at the top of the dog's neck and steadies Copper's head with his other hand after the judge has finished going over it. He may at this time give Copper a piece of bait to nibble on to keep Copper's attention facing forward. To accomplish the second, Taran moves—as smoothly and as simply as possible—to be where the judge is not.

The judge examines the dog on the table. Note how Andrew holds the head steady with his fingers tucked under the jawbone so they cannot be seen in profile.

Moving a Foot

Even in the conformation ring a judge might move a dog's foot to an incorrect position to see if the dog will replace it correctly because he is made correctly. This is unusual, however, and a judge who moves a foot is more likely to do so because it was incorrectly placed.

The same is true in the American Kennel Club junior handling rings. Unless it is clearly incorrect, the handler should note what the judge does and use that placement thereafter with that judge.

In Canadian Kennel club shows, the judge may move a dog's foot to test the handler's knowledge of the correct placement and to test the handler's ability to replace it correctly.

To replace a front foot, Taran shifts the Copper's weight to the foot he is not going to move either by a light pull on the leash or by moving his head. Then when the weight is shifted, he moves the foot, grasping the leg at about the shoulder. If it is the leg on the side opposite him that needs to be moved, he does not lean over Copper, but reaches underneath or moves in front of Copper to make the correction.

To replace a rear foot, Taran shifts the weight and grasps the leg at the hock, again reaching underneath to get to a foot on his opposite side.

If Copper has replaced his foot correctly himself, Taran visibly checks to be sure it is correct.

The Moving Judge in Examinations

Judges in Canadian Kennel Club shows move unpredictably to test the handler's alertness and the handler's ability to keep the dog always between the judge and the handler. In these shows Taran is quick to move to the opposite side of Copper but never steps over him. He can then smile at the judge—a quick "I did it" kind of smile.

In the top picture, judge Michelle Yeadon has started to move behind the juniors. Joellen Dilay with the Nova Scotia Duck Tolling Retriever, Tollwest Mystical Wave, has already moved; Ashley Gold with the Havanese, Can. Ch. Misty Trails Harry Potter by Emmy, is beginning to shift, and Sarah Turner with the powderpuff Chinese Crested, "B B" and Brittany Mowatt with the miniature Dachshund, Neuenrade's I'm All That Ms. is watching alertly. In the bottom picture, Joellen has shifted completely to the opposite side of the judge and the other three girls have completed moving also.

9

Patterns and Turns

After the judge has examined Copper individually, he will have Taran move the dog in one or more patterns so that he can observe the dog's gait from front, rear, and side. Taran listens closely to the judge's directions, and asks for an explanation if he does not understand. He has also watched the dogs and handlers ahead of him. However, the handlers ahead of him may have been incorrect, or the judge may want to change the directions for Taran, so Taran should not follow earlier handlers blindly. If at any time during the individual gaiting Copper bounces, pulls, or otherwise moves incorrectly, Taran stops and corrects him and may even go back to the corner and start over. He gives the judge every opportunity to see Copper's gait at its best. He does not cut the corners, but he does slow down slightly to give Copper a chance to steady himself. Unless the judge tells him to move in a circle, Taran moves in a straight line to do all patterns. The judge ordinarily uses the same pattern on every dog. When he was learnng the patterns, Taran practised first with a stuffed dog on the end of a leash so that he would not confuse Copper.

The Honor

The honor (some people call this a courtesy turn, but here I save that term for the courtesy turn done at the end of the ring) is used as a part of almost every gaiting pattern. To honor the judge, Taran pivots clockwise, keeping Copper on the outside, and ends up with Copper pointed in the direction that they are going to travel. Its purpose is to give Copper a chance to move smoothly for the entire length of the ring, rather than spend part of the space straightening himself out.

Courtesy Turn

At the end of the diagonal, the handler and dog may simply turn and come back. To do this smoothly, use a courtesy turn (sometimes called a "blind" courtesy turn to distinguish it from the honor.) In the courtesy turn, Taran moves straight into position, but swings Copper into a small clockwise circle, ending with both facing in the direction of travel.

In the left-hand picture, Bert Johnson swings his Norwegian Elkhound, Sir Studly of Paradise, in a circle to begin the honor before starting on the diagonal. In the right, the dog is straightened out and ready to begin the diagonal.

In the left picture Julie Despot makes a courtesy turn. She swings her Golden Retriever Shayla in a circle away from her body. In the right picture, she has almost completed the turn and she and Shayla are ready to move.

Some handlers advise against doing a courtesy turn with large or heavy-moving dogs. In the conformation ring it may be better to skip the courtesy turn in those circumstances; in junior showmanship competition, use the courtesy turn. Practice until you and the dog learns to do it smoothly.

Gaiting Patterns

There are several gaiting patterns that a judge might use. I will discuss first the ones used in both American and Canadian Kennel Club shows and then go on to the more complicated patterns called for by some Canadian Kennel Club judges. If Taran is showing at an indoor ring, he has a mat to guide him; in an outdoor ring he needs to use the ring barriers to keep himself moving in a straight line.

Down and Back

When Copper goes up the diagonal away from the judge, the judge can see how Copper moves in the rear. Taran has someone watch him while he practices to find what Copper's best speed is. When Copper is coming back toward the judge, the judge looks at Copper's forward movement. With these principles in mind, Taran understands that he must move Copper smoothly and in a straight line up and down with Copper lined up with the judge.

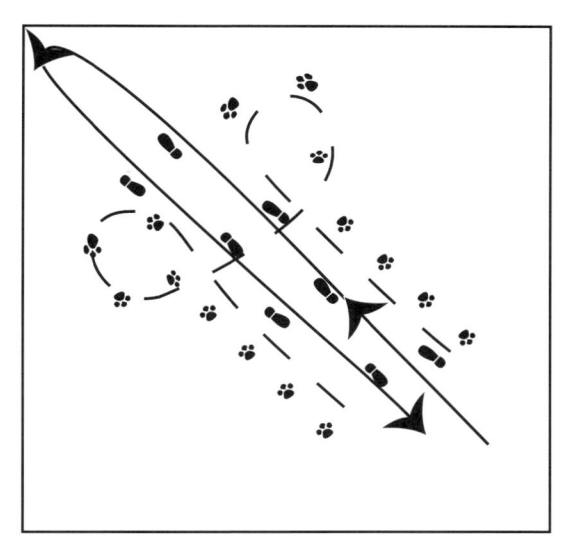

Diagram 1: Courtesy turn

Kyle Bull stops his Samoyed, Am/Can. Ch. Sancha's Vintage White Whine, a good distance from the judge. Note how Kyle has stepped back to give the judge a clear view of the dog. To get a good expression from the dog, he holds the bait in his right hand.

Return to Line

Now the judge needs to study Copper's movement from the side, so he will send Taran around the ring where Taran will finish up at the end of the line of dogs. Taran honors the judge again and moves straight up the side of the ring. He follows the line of the ring. As he reaches the place where he will stop, leaving good spacing between his dog and the one ahead of him, he slows down and turns to face Copper, again allowing him to free stack. If the judge is watching, he baits Copper.

While he is standing close to the corner of the diagonal he is aware that the judge's eye may fall on Copper at any time and keeps Copper in a good stack.

Sean has just returned to his position in line after completing a pattern. He has pivoted into position and allowed his dog to assume a natural stack.

Note that the Basset in the corner is in the judge's line of sight as the Sheltie reaches that spot. Therefore the Basset in particular should be in a good show stack. The ones further away may be more relaxed.

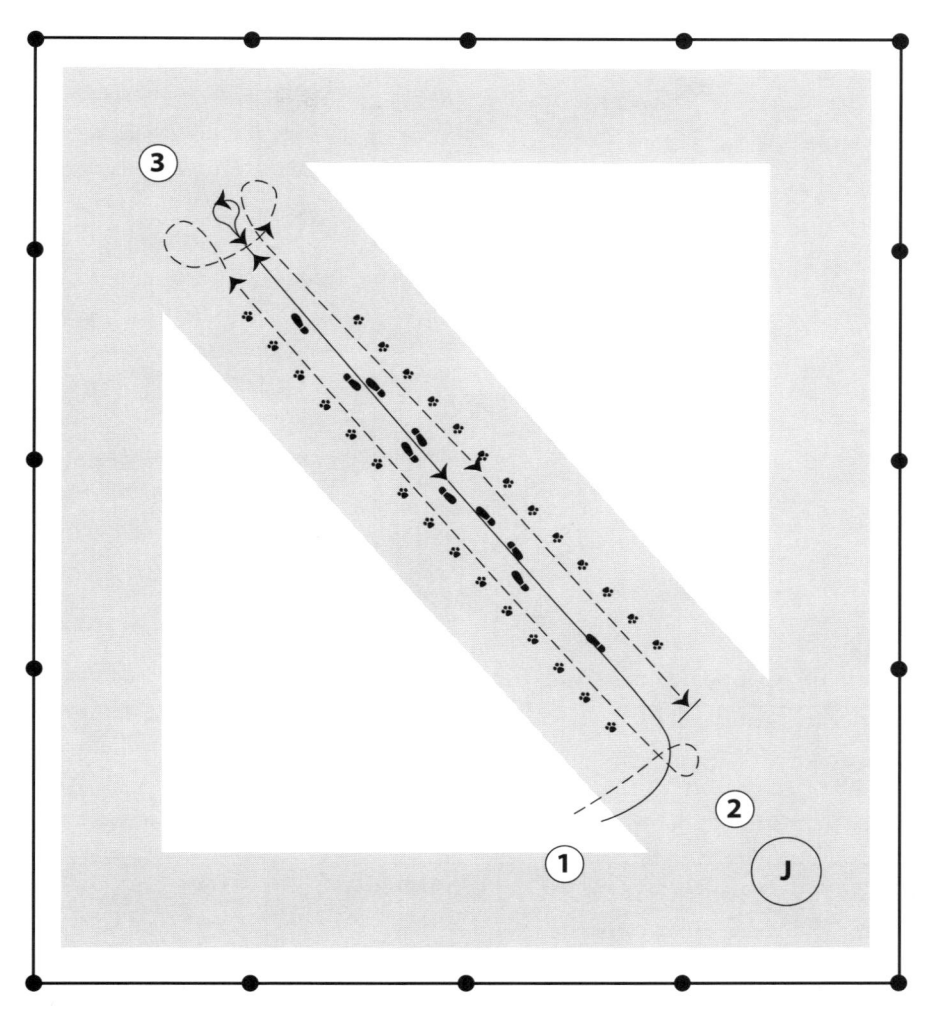

Diagram 2: Both directions of diagonal. The basic pattern seems simple—take the dog up and back on the diagonal. This pattern begins at (1) with Copper standing where he was when the judge finished examining him. Taran lifts Copper from the table, puts him carefully on the ground, and comes forward until he is opposite the judge. (2)There he honors the judge, bringing Copper back directly in front of the judge and aimed at the opposite corner of the diagonal. (Handlers who show their dogs on ramps lead the dog down the ramp, and then continue as described; handlers who start their dogs on the ground lead them in front of the judge and then make their honor.)

Taran moves Copper at his best speed to the corner of the diagonal (3) , makes a courtesy turn so that Copper faces the judge, moves him straight back down the diagonal and stops (2) facing the judge. (The rule of thumb for how far away from the judge to stop is, if you fell flat on your face when you stopped, you would just touch the judge's shoes.) When Taran stops, he lets Copper come into a natural stance, shifting his weight with the leash as necessary to straighten his feet. Taran pivots on his left foot so that he stands off to Copper's side, leaving Copper facing straight forward looking at the judge.

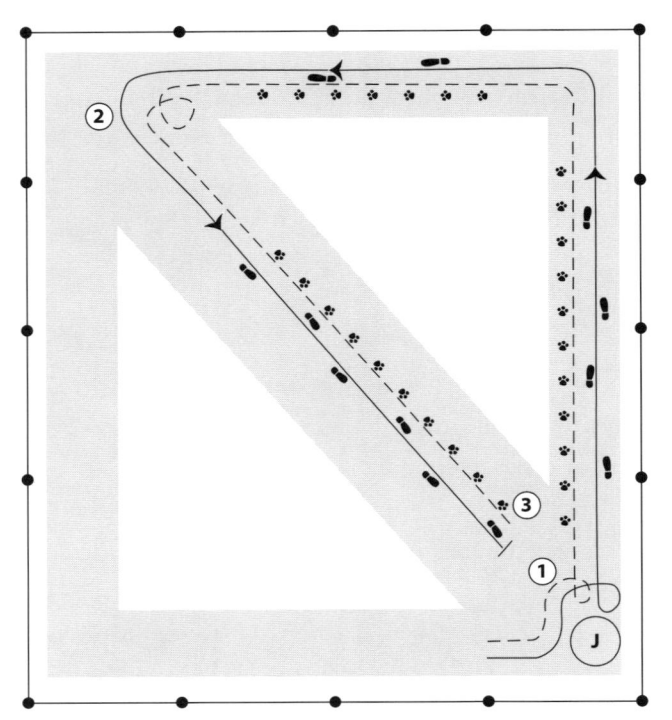

The Triangle

Some judges prefer the triangle, which is more economical of time in viewing the dog's movement. If the judge calls for this pattern, just as in doing the diagonal Taran honors the judge (1), who is standing at the side of the ring (J). Taran goes down the side and across the back of the ring, makes a courtesy turn at the acute angle of the triangle (2), and then comes back down the diagonal, stopping as shown in the diagonal pattern description (3).

The L

The L is a pattern used by some Canadian Kennel Club judges. The first half is done like the first part of the triangle, but then, instead of returning on the diagonal, (1) Taran reverses his direction and comes back to the judge the same way that he went away, tracing an upside-down L. Now comes the problem. When Taran turns to retrace his steps, Copper is on the wrong side. On Taran's left, Copper is between Taran and the ring barriers. Taran must change hands and move Copper along the back of the ring on his right side. When he gets to the corner, (2) he changes hands again and comes down to ring to (3). If Taran competes in Canadian shows, he must train Copper to move on his right side as well as on his left.

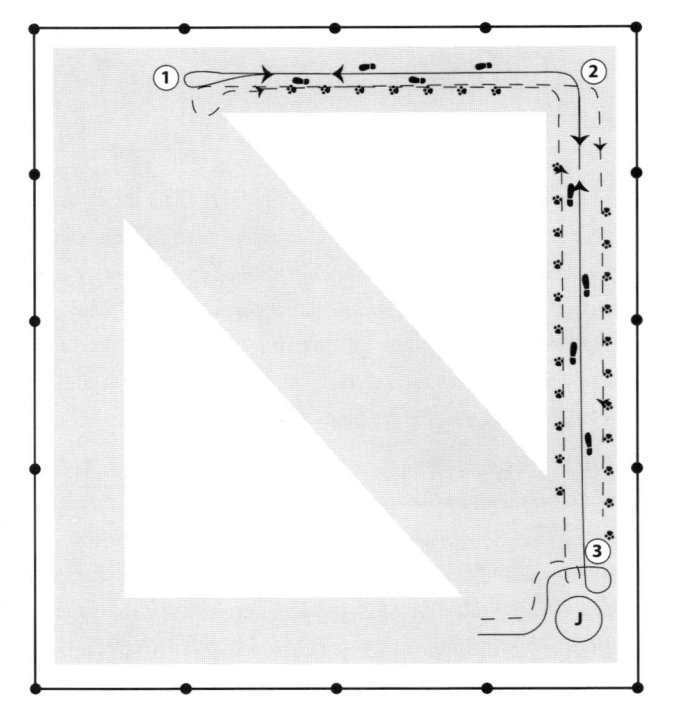

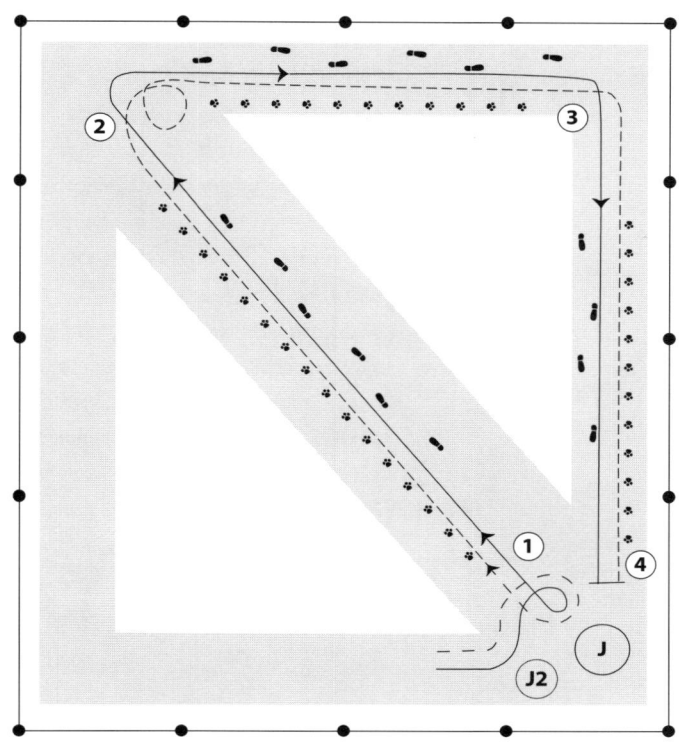

The Backwards Triangle

The backwards triangle starts on the diagonal (1) with an honor in front of the judge (J) and finishes coming straight down the side of the ring. At the top of the diagonal (2) Taran will make a courtesy turn and change hands. At the next corner (3) he will change hands again and come down the ring and stop facing the judge. WARNING: Look at where the judge is when starting down the last leg of the triangle. If the judge has moved to the left, (J2), do not change hands at (3), but take the dog down the last leg on the right side.

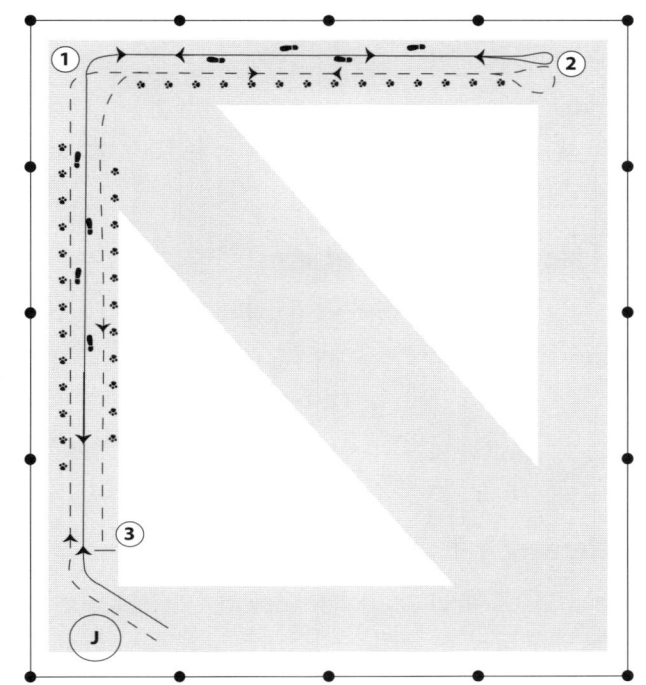

The Backwards L

The backwards L may start at the far left of the ring or at the center. When Taran reaches the back corner of the ring (1), he will turn right, making a courtesy turn and changing hands, and go completely to the right side (2). There he will make a courtesy turn, change hands again, and retrace his steps to (3).

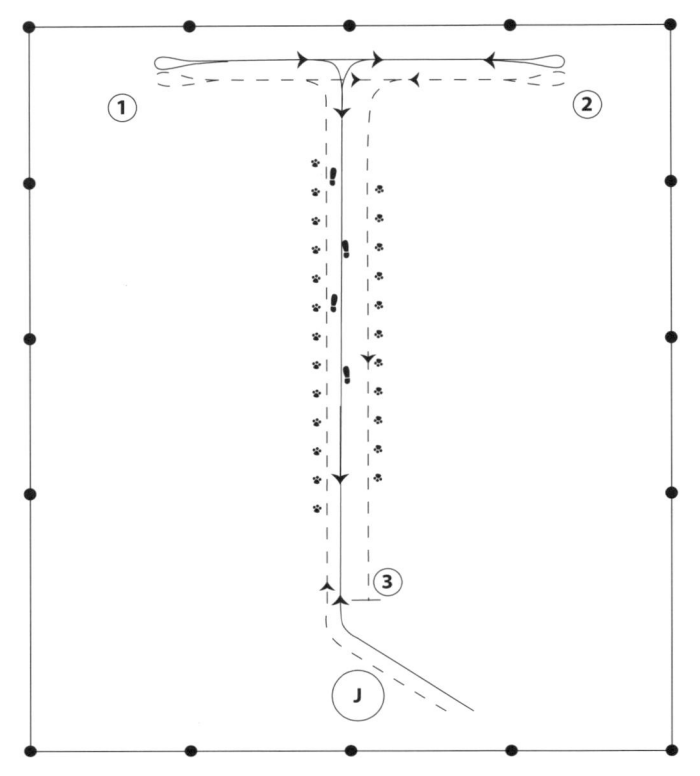

The T

The T starts in the center of the ring. Unless the judge tells him otherwise, Taran goes straight up the center of the ring, turns left, and goes to the corner (1). There he makes a courtesy turn and changes hands and goes to the opposite corner (2). He makes a courtesy turn and changes hands, goes to the center of the ring and turns and comes straight down the center to the judge (3). Whether he will make a courtesy turn at the top of the T and change hands again will depend on where the judge is standing at the time he reaches this point.

Changing Hands

Taran learns to change hands smoothly. To change hands on the lead, as Taran makes the turn at the end of the ring, he brings both hands together in front of him and transfers the leash to the other hand.

The Moving Judge in Patterns

One more problem that a Canadian Kennel Club judge may set before Taran is to move while Taran is following a pattern. In order to have Copper correctly positioned between himself and the judge, whenever Taran comes to a corner he takes a quick glance to be sure that when he turns he will not be between Copper and the judge, and makes whatever changes are necessary.

Difference in Philosophy in Use of Patterns

Canadian Kennel Club rules permit—in fact, encourage—judges to use more difficult patterns that are not ordinarily used in the conformation ring. Until recently the American

Kennel Club also allowed the use of difficult patterns, but its present rules do not. (It is possible, although unlikely, that a judge who began judging under the old rules might use such a pattern. In that case, Taran would say nothing and follow the judge's directions.)

The argument in favor of using only the patterns employed in the conformation ring and of having the judge move only as necessary is: why expect from junior handlers skills that they will never use in real-life handling? A further difficulty with the use of complicated patterns is that in mastering them the juniors may lose track of the basics.

The argument in favor of a complicated handling pattern and of a moving judge is that the best handler is the least conspicuous. Therefore the ideal handler is the one whom the judge remembers least. The judge should be thinking, "What a gorgeous dog!" not "What a clever handler!" Since all the dogs in the class are not equally show-worthy, the judge is not working from a level playing field. Therefore, judging on handling skills allows handlers to show what they know and can do with their dogs. The judge has a more objective set of skills by which to measure the handler.

Miscellaneous Information

10

Bad Weather

Handlers at outdoor shows must contend with the weather. The weather can be too cold, too hot, and rainy.

Most dogs are hardy enough to survive and show in any degree of cold weather that is reasonably likely to occur at an outdoor show. Taran may slip on an extra sweater under his jacket if it is super cold, and he keeps Copper warmly wrapped until it is time to go into the ring.

Rainy weather poses no problem for short-coated breeds. Long-coated breeds need to be kept as dry as possible so that their coats look good. Taran follows the judge's example as to whether or not to wear rain gear into the ring. He makes sure that he is wearing shoes that will not slip on the wet surface underfoot.

Hot weather more common. Again Taran follows the judge's example as to what to wear and whether to remove his jacket or tie. His protection of Copper is his chief concern. He has water available for him to drink and may carry a water bottle into the ring. If he does not have deep enough pockets he leaves the bottle outside the ring opening or has someone else there to hand it to him. He covers Copper with a cool damp cloth or sprays him with cool water or both whenever he can and keeps him in whatever shade is available. Since dogs do not perspire as people do, the important areas to spray are the stomach, the undersides of the paws, and beneath the tail. He watches for any signs of problems—heavy panting, lolling tongue, trembling—and removes Copper from the ring if necessary to protect his well-being. Taran will need to be especially careful if he shows a dog with a black coat or a dog with a pushed-in nose such as a Boxer, a Pekinese, or a Bulldog, since these are the types most endangered by heat.

Tents

If the show is outdoors and the weather is hot or rainy, there will probably be a tent under which the exhibitors can wait until it is time to show their dogs. Judges may divide the class and send exhibitors to the tent, either in or out of the ring, or they may conduct the individual examinations under the tent. When gaiting Copper, Taran never goes under the tent unless specifically told to do so by the judge.

Working in Pairs

Working in pairs is discouraged, but not forbidden in American Kennel Club shows. It is used in competition where a judge wants to compare the gait of two dogs, but it does present a safety issue since the dogs are working close together. When dogs work in pairs, they are moved across the ring side by side with the handlers on the outside. It is not a race—each handler should move his dog at its best speed, but still try to keep the dogs close enough that the judge can compare them. When they get to the end of the ring, Taran turns Copper away from the other dog to avoid a face-to-face encounter. He pivots in place and changes hands on the leash. The two dogs start together back to the judge.

The two Norwegian Elkhounds are being gaited in pairs so the judge can compare their gaits. Note that in the first picture, going away from the judge, the dog with Bert, the taller boy, is on his left, while the second dog is on Sean's right. As they return to the judge in the second picture, the dogs are still together, but their positions in relation to their handlers are reversed. Sean has allowed his dog to get slightly ahead—the dogs should be kept as close together as possible.

Exchanging Dogs

There are obvious safety issues for both dogs and handlers when the handlers exchange dogs in the ring. For this reason American Kennel Club forbids the practice and the Canadian Kennel Club limits it to Senior Open classes and zone finals. However, it is an excellent way for a judge to find out whether the handler is good or the dog is simply showing itself, as well as to see what the junior knows about handling breeds not his own. The best preparation for Taran is to watch other breeds being shown and learn their fine points, and if possible to handle them for other people. When Taran reaches the point of exchanging dogs in the ring, he will be careful to keep the dogs being exchanged separate from each other.

Judge's Questions

In Canadian Kennel Club shows the judges are encouraged to ask questions to test the handlers' knowledge. The questions may be:

- About the handler's breed: "What is your breed used for?" "In what country did your breed originate?"
- About breeds in general: "In what group is the Lhasa Apso?"
- About dog anatomy: "Where are the withers?" "Where is the dog's collarbone?" (That last was a trick question—dogs don't have collarbones.) The questions will be the same for every handler. If the question asks Taran to locate a body part, he keeps the hand that points it out concealed from the other handlers.

In 4-H junior showmanship events, the questions by the judge are usually required and are more likely to focus upon canine anatomy, since not all 4-H handlers have purebred dogs. They may include general 4-H information as well.

Bait and Toys

Although bait and toys are used in the ring to get a sparkling expression from the dog, they should not be obvious. Bait is used in several ways. The bait Taran uses is a food treat that Copper particularly likes. Good choices for most dogs are cubes of cheese, small pieces of chicken, or slices of liver cooked with garlic or anise. This is not a feeding session—the pieces of bait, even for large dogs, are no larger than a nickel. Crunchy treats are not a good choice as dogs may leave crumbs. Squeaky or furry toys are also good attention-getters for some dogs and traditional in certain breeds. Handlers who use them must avoid distracting other dogs.

Taran leaves no trace of his bait behind. He never throws it on the ground and does not allow Copper to eat any bait that others have dropped.

Above: Sandy Shamblin is rewarding her Welsh terrier at the end of a pattern. It is important to reward the dog from time to time when he is being baited in the other ways described here, so that he always believes that the bait will be given to him. Handlers who use bait as a reward must be careful that the dog does not think he is being rewarded for breaking his stack.

Christine DeForest free baits her Great Dane, Bliss, and he follows her hand with the bait into a correct stack.

Above: Chelsea Birmingham is feeding her Golden Retriever Trevor to keep his mind occupied while judge Michelle Yeadon examines his rear. Handlers who use it in this way must be sure to be ready for the next thing that the judge will ask them to do.

Right: Taran keeps his bait in his pocket and Copper looks at him alertly whenever his hand moves in that direction. In front of him Christa Eussen with her Japanese Chin, Keiko, also uses bait to keep her dog alert. She holds it high so that her dog looks up and displays high-flying ears. Handlers who use bait in this way must hold the bait so that the dog holds his head in the right position for the breed.

"Selling" the Dog

As a beginner, Taran works on improving his handling skills. When he has those down pat, he begins to study his dog. He reads books on his breed and talks to breeders, judges, and handlers. He learns what are Copper's best features and how to make the most of them. He also learns Copper's faults—and all dogs have them—and finds ways to minimize them. He subtly shows the good points to the judge in what is called "fingerwork." He may lightly touch a

Note how Christine's left hand draws the judge's eye to her Great Dane's good topline. Behind her, Robyn McKim's hand calls attention to the nicely curved stifle of her Whippet, Castlecrest's Silver and Gold.

good head or frame it with his fingers, smooth his hand across a good topline, place Copper toward the edge of the mat nearest the ring to emphasize a good front, catch the judge's eye while gaiting to emphasize his dog's gait. He does not do this more than once—the judge saw it the first time. On the other hand, some judges tell a class at the outset that they do not want to see any "tricks." In that case, Taran omits all fingerwork and may also skip courtesy turns.

Misbehavior

Taran should not try to show Copper until he is sure that he can control him. If Copper acts up for any reason, Taran keeps working with him to steady him. He stays calm and patient because he knows that often a handler who is trying hard with a difficult dog will impress the judge favorably. If the misbehavior is so bad that the judge excuses him, he leaves quietly without comment. If this behavior is unusual for Copper, he checks him for physical problems. He thinks back over what happened before and in the ring to try to find the cause of the problem. Then he lets Copper do one thing that he knows how to do and likes to do, and rewards and plays with him so that they finish on a good note.

Even though bitches in season are forbidden in the junior showmanship ring, there may have been one there earlier, leaving her delectable scent for Copper, who is an intact male. If Taran knows or suspects this to be the case, he swipes a quick dash of vanilla or mentholatum under Copper's nose before they enter the ring.

At an outdoor show if there are bugs about, Taran uses an insect repellant that is safe for dogs on himself and on Copper, being careful to spray Copper's underbelly thoroughly, before taking him in the ring.

Two in the Family

Two juniors from the same family who are both showing in juniors may help each other or show real sibling rivalry or—usually—both. Outside the ring, the parents need to be careful not to compare one against the other or put too much responsibility on the older to help the younger. It is important to remind a younger child who is outshining the older sibling that the younger had a running start in learning from the older child's experience. Encourage each child to develop individual goals. One parent told me that the chief problem of his two daughters in the ring was that each concentrated on watching her sister instead of her dog.

If both will be in the ring together, whether in conformation or in junior showmanship, if they have similar dogs and the more closely the two resemble each other physically, the more important it is to be sure that they are outstandingly different in dress. I saw one case where the judge got confused in a puppy sweepstakes class and pointed to the wrong one of two sisters for just this reason. In Junior Showmanship it is probably better to have the two showing different breeds if this is possible.

Young and Cute

A problem for some juniors, particularly those who start showing very young in Pee Wee classes and the like, is that they are cute. They are overly praised for their handling skills, which are perhaps truly remarkable for a young child, and they and their parents begin to think that they are destined for greatness. These children and their parents may get their first shock when they enter a stiff regular Novice class, or it may not be until they hit the Open class that they learn that there are others out there just as good, if not better. Since the children are too young to maintain good balance, it is up to the parents to keep a clear head during the "cute" period so that the child will not be discouraged when reality sets in.

Challenges Ahead

As Taran gains in skill and begins to win regularly in the Open class, he may set himself further challenges. Many juniors aim at showing in the shows that are exclusively for the top winners. It is hard to treat such competition with the calm of "just another show." But the junior who overrates its importance will lose forever the fun of showing in such an environment and have at best a fleeting win and at worst a lasting disappointment.

Restricted Entry Shows

Restricted* entry shows are open only to juniors who have won a number of Open classes within about a year before the date of the show. They may also be further limited to junior handlers who live in a particular area or who have qualified at shows held within a particular geographical area. The show-giving club decides how many wins are necessary to qualify, whether geographic limitations apply, and what are the precise dates of the qualification period. In most cases only wins against competition are counted in determining eligibility. These classes will of course be highly competitive.

A junior who "ages out"—that is, becomes too old to compete further in junior showmanship—between the date that the junior qualifies and the date of the restricted entry show, is still eligible to compete. It is the junior's age at the date of the qualification that is important.

The eligibility requirements for the dog are the same as those for all other Junior Showmanship classes.

Westminster Kennel Club

Perhaps the best known of the restricted entry shows is that held by the Westminster Kennel Club on the second Monday and Tuesday in February. The number of wins necessary to qualify has grown steadily over the years and to be eligible for the 2005 show the

---

* The American Kennel Club uses the term "limited entry" to refer both to shows that are limited in the number of dogs that can be entered and to shows whose entrants must meet certain higher standards. To avoid confusion, I use the term "limited" to mean limited in number and the term "restricted" to mean limited by requirements.

juniors must have ten wins in Open class with competition between December 2, 2003, and November 11, 2004. Even at this requirement level, the entries are limited to 100. Although Westminster is an American Kennel Club event, juniors who are residents of other countries but have the requisite number of wins at American Kennel Club shows are eligible to compete.

Adult male handlers may wear tuxedos and women handlers wear formal or semiformal clothes that still allow them to move freely. Juniors should wear clothes of the same level of formality suitable to their age and maturity. Although it is midwinter, the combination of bright lights and shoulder-to-shoulder crowds make Westminster overly warm for both dogs and handlers.

Westminster is a two-day show, with half the groups showing on Monday and the other half, plus Best in Show, on Tuesday. The juniors show in preliminary classes on the same day as that for their breed. No placements are made but four top contenders are chosen on each day. These compete for Best Junior prior to the Best in Show judging.

Because Westminster is second only to the Kentucky Derby as the longest running United States sporting event; because not only is the Junior Showmanship limited but also the conformation entries, being open only to American Kennel Club champions; because it is held in the United States' largest city; and because it has traditionally received wide media coverage, Westminster is considered as the American "Show of Shows," and a win there earns the crown of Best in whatever category.

Eukanuba Invitational

The Eukanuba National Invitational Championship requires not only proficiency as a handler but also classroom ability. In 2004, juniors must have had within the competition year five wins with competition present in an Open class and in addition a grade point average of 3.0 or better, or the equivalent, for the two semesters completed immediately before the closing of entries. The GPA must be verified by an official school transcript or home school information sent in and received by the American Kennel Club before they send the entry form to the junior.

As with Westminster, the juniors compete in preliminary classes, from which the judges select a specified number to compete in finals. Again like Westminster, no placements are made in the preliminary classes.

Canadian Zonal Competitions

The Canadian Kennel Club, unlike the American Kennel Club, selects the country's top junior handler of the year. The Provincial/Zone Junior Handling competitions are held once a year to choose a Best Junior Handler for each of the Canadian Kennel Club provinces/zones. The winners of these compete at National Junior Handling competitions for the title of Top Canadian Junior Handler.

Juniors receive 100 points for first place wins from Open class, 75 for second place, 50 for third place, and 25 for fourth place. These wins are tabulated and compiled according to the province/zone in which the junior lives, regardless of the province/zone in which the win was made. At the end of the calendar year in each province/zone, the top five juniors at each level—Novice Junior, Novice Senior, Open Junior, and Open Senior—as determined by the accumulated points, compete sometime before August 31 to represent the province/zone in the National competition. If there is a tie in the scores, all juniors with that score may compete. At the zone competition there are a minimum of three judges—one to set ring procedure and the other two to observe. A winner and a reserve winner are chosen, and if the winner cannot go to National to compete, the reserve winner may go.

At the National competition, the judging is also done by a panel of three judges. The classes are not divided, and the handlers may be asked to exchange dogs.

Other Challenges

Not all juniors, for one reason or another, can compete in these select shows. But good young handlers can still show and improve their skills in or outside the junior showmanship ring. Taran's Aunt Kathy challenged herself to win Best Junior with one dog from each group. In addition she worked with a brace, and won Best Brace in Show with them, as well as Highest Scoring Brace in obedience competition. Taran's Uncle Robert handled dogs for other people as often as he had the opportunity. He did not expect to get paid while he was still learning.

Robert poses a long-haired Dachshund that he showed for a woman who could not get to the Fairbanks show. She paid Rob's airfare from Anchorage.

Here Kathy shows our black-and-tan Cockers, Panache Miss Jean Brodie and Panache Prime Time, to win best brace in show. Kathy taught the two dogs to move in absolute synchronized step, so that from a profile it was hard to tell that there were two dogs.

12

Wrapping It Up

Winning and Losing

Just as competition does not begin at the point when Taran enters the ring, but rather with his preparation, the competition does not end when the ribbons are handed out. Taran tries to follow the motto that his great-grandfather taught: "Win without bragging; lose without excuses." If he is not the winner of the class, he congratulates the person who did win.

When it is convenient for the judge, he asks if the judge can offer any suggestions to improve his performance. He never argues with the judge or asks, "Why didn't I win?" At the very worst, he remembers that all that happened was that he received one person's opinion on one day. If he really felt that the judge was unfair or incompetent, he may decide not to show under that judge again. Even when he wins, he may want to ask the judge for suggestions, not only to find ways to improve but to know what particularly impressed the judge. Taran placed in the ribbons at his first show because the judge was so impressed by the extreme care that he took lifting Copper on and off the table.

If he is the winner, Taran will probably want to get his picture taken by the show photographer of him and his dog with the judge. These pictures are regularly scheduled and all judges make time for them. Taran makes sure that the picture shows him and his dog to the best advantage. Although there is a cost, they make a fine memory of the day.

Whether he wins or loses, he gives Copper a quick bit of play and reward.

Keeping a Record

Taran keeps a record of every show and match in which he competes. He notes any problems he had with Copper, any successful moves that he tried, and any comments made by the judge or other knowledgeable people. Record forms are on the last pages of this book.

Basic Rules

Taran knows that his first concern must always be for Copper's safety and comfort. When he shows Copper to the judge he treats him like a precious and beautiful object. In the ring he is always careful to listen to and to watch the judge. He practices courtesy in the ring to the other handlers and, of course, the judge.

No-No's

There are a few don'ts that Taran has learned to observe:
- He never comes between Copper and the judge or lets anything else do so.
- He does not talk to the judge before or during the judging except where it is absolutely necessary. However, if he does not understand what the judge tells him to do, he asks to have it repeated.
- He does not talk to other handlers in the ring.
- He does not talk to or even look at anyone outside the ring except in an emergency.
- Taran never fusses over Copper. He sets him up with as few moves as possible and keeps him set up without over-handling.
- He never lets Copper touch or sniff another dog.
- Even if Taran shows a long-coated dog, in the ring he does only whatever grooming is absolutely necessary.
- Taran never scolds or jerks Copper in or out of the ring.

Winning Tips

As he progresses in his handling, Taran learns handling procedures that make him and Copper a winning team.

Taran learns to develop his eye for a correct stack. He looks at Copper from above when Copper is stacked correctly on the ground to see exactly what he looks like. He sets a timer when he practices stacking and tries to do everything necessary in less than ten seconds. Handler Penny King recommends that Taran practice stacking Copper in front of a covered mirror. Then the cover is removed and Taran can see if he did it right.

Taran learns to move at Copper's best speed.
- A good way to learn this is to have someone who knows the breed watch him until he gets it just right. Then he finds a song that matches that speed and hums it under his breath to keep himself and Copper at the right speed.
- To practice moving smoothly Taran practices with a penny on his head so that he learns to hold his head up straight. To keep his leash-holding hand from moving, in practice he holds a spoon with a penny in it.
- One way to look smooth in movement is to move in step with the dog. Not all handlers can do this with all dogs; it depends on their relative size. If the handler and dog move naturally at about the same speed, step out with the same foot that the dog uses.

See how smooth Meghan and her dog, Am/Can/ Int Ch. Heartwood's Jewel of WM Wranch, CGC, WAC, appear as they move in step.

Taran watches the judge at any classes that are ahead of his so that he can see what patterns and variations the judge uses. He watches other junior handlers with this judge and tries to see what particular skills and actions are most important to this judge.

As Taran gains more ring experience he learns to size up his judges before he goes into the ring and to modify his handling style slightly to suit. If he has kept careful notes, he may know that a judge likes or dislikes certain optional behavior and is careful to follow the judge's preference as much as possible. Although this is a generalization only, Taran expects judges who were or are handlers to look for flashier behavior than do judges who also judge regularly in the breed ring.

Taran learns to smile at the judge. He does not grin or flirt, but he does smile confidently when he enters the ring—after all, he is giving the judge the opportunity to see a truly beautiful dog! He also smiles confidently again when he brings Copper down in front of the judge. If the judge has asked him for a difficult handling maneuver, he smiles when he has completed it to let the judge know that he has done it right, and knows he was right.

Taran pays attention in the ring not only to the judge and to Copper but to the dogs in front of and behind him. He is constantly alert to what is happening.

Taran and Copper will work together over the years, growing in companionship and in understanding of each other. Whether Taran ends up as a Best Junior Handler in one of the top dog shows of the year or simply learns to compete in events that teach him valuable life skills, he gains. Together he and Copper are a winning team.

Appendix 1: American Kennel Club Rules and Regulation

Reprinted by permission of the American Kennel Club. These regulations are abridged to omit technicalities of importance only to judges or show-giving clubs.

A Guide to Junior Showmanship Competition for Juniors

Section 1. Amateur Class

An individual listed as an agent is not eligible to compete in Juniors, nor any person who distributes rate cards or otherwise advertises themselves as handling dogs for pay in the show ring, or accepts payment for handling dogs.

Participation in Junior Showmanship is intended to encourage Juniors to learn how to care for and present different breeds. Part of the educational process could include apprenticeship or assisting professional handlers. Junior may take their employers' dogs into the ring while still retaining amateur status.

Section 2.

Juniors are important to the sport of dogs. Juniors who learn about good sportsmanship, dogs, handling, and dog shows will be valuable to the sport in the future. Junior Showmanship classes are offered at most dog shows. These classes are held so that young people can:

- Experience winning and losing among those who are similar in age.
- Learn the correct way to handle the breed they own.
- Practice handling skills in competition.
- Improve the way they handle their own dog.
- Prepare for handling dogs in the regular classes.

Section 3.

Junior Showmanship classes are judged on the ability of the Junior to handle his or her dog. The quality of the dog is not judged. Juniors will be asked to demonstrate:

- Moving the dog with the rest of the class.

- Presenting the dog in the standing position proper to its breed (including the use of an examining table for those breeds normally judged on a table).
- Moving the dog individually in a regular pattern.

Section 4.

Juniors are expected to know basic ring routines. They should be able to follow directions, use space wisely, and be familiar with gaiting patterns. Juniors should appear "ring wise," alert to what is going on in the ring, and should be prepared for changes in the routine of judging.

JUNIORS MUST BE ABLE TO CONTROL THEIR DOGS AT ALL TIMES. Any Junior who cannot control his or her dog will be excused by the judge.

Section 5. Appearance and Conduct

Juniors should be clean, neat, and well-groomed. They should wear clothing that is comfortable to handle in and appropriate for dog shows. Clothing should not distract, limit, or hinder the judge's view of the dog.

Dogs should be groomed and trimmed as they would be for the breed ring. Judges will not evaluate the quality of the grooming and trimming, but Juniors should make an effort to prepare their dogs properly. Unnecessary grooming of the dog in the ring to gain attention is not proper conduct.

Juniors should appear confident, prepared, business-like and attentive. They should be courteous to both the judge and other Juniors. Juniors are expected to handle their dogs without disturbing the dogs of the other Juniors. Juniors should not crowd and they should not distract others by continued use of toys and bait. Juniors should be alert to the needs of their dogs. They should use firm but thoughtful hands in controlling and handling their dogs. Juniors should not be impatient or heavy-handed.

Section 6. Conflicts.

Juniors may have a conflict between the Judging of their Junior Showmanship class and conformation judging or another event. In this instance the Junior will have to make a decision as to where they will compete. A Junior may enter the Junior Showmanship class up until the time every Junior in the class has been examined and gaited. If a Junior starts to compete in the Junior class and requests to be excused to go exhibit in conformation or another event, he or she is permanently excused.

Section 7.

Juniors will be judged on their ability to present their dogs in the same way the dog is properly handled in the breed ring. Juniors will also be judged on their ability to make their individual dog look its best in both pose and motion. During all parts of the competition, Juniors should handle their dogs in a quiet, smooth, efficient manner. Juniors should strive to make the *dog* stand out as the most important part of the team effort.

Section 8.

Junior handlers should:
- Keep their dog's attention without using dramatic or unnecessary movements.
- Gait their dogs in a controlled trot without distracting or interfering with the judge's view of the dog. Be aware of what is going on in the ring.
- Concentrate on their dog and not the judge.
- Junior handlers who use exaggerated posture, motions, or gestures in any part of the competition will be faulted.

Section 9.

There are many ways Juniors can find help in learning about Junior Showmanship and handling their own dogs. In addition to the help of parents, Juniors may seek the advice of experienced breeder-exhibitors, professional handlers, handling instructors, and former Juniors. They may also learn from the AKC breed videocassettes, books on handling, books on individual breeds, and by observing breed and group judging at dog shows.

Section 10. Substitution.

Juniors are limited to the substitution of one dog per show. The junior must have the AKC number of the substitute dog.

Junior Showmanship Judging Guidelines

Section 1. Definition and Purpose.

Junior Showmanship classes are nonregular classes which are judged solely on the ability and skill of Juniors in handling their dogs as in the breed ring. The purpose of Junior Showmanship Competition is twofold: to introduce and encourage Juniors to participate in the sport of dogs and to provide Juniors with a meaningful competition in which they can learn, practice, and improve in all areas of handling skill and sportsmanship. It is important that judges of Junior Showmanship competition understand the definition and purpose of these classes and take seriously their role in guiding the future guardians of the sport. JUDGES ARE EXPECTED TO HAVE A GENUINE INTEREST IN JUNIORS AND IN JUNIOR SHOWMANSHIP COMPETITION.

Section 4. Responsibilities of the Junior Showmanship Judge.

It is important for judges to be teachers by example. They should be prompt, courteous, patient, and properly attired. Judges must be impartial and totally separate the handling ability of the Juniors they judge from any other consideration. As a judge of Juniors at an all-breed event, it is essential to be familiar with the appropriate presentation for every breed. Impartiality extends to eliminating from the judging process bias for or against the breed handled, friendships, external knowledge of a Junior's record of competition, or prior knowledge or assumption of the dog's training or preparation.

If a Junior co-owns a dog with a judge, the dog may be entered in Junior Showmanship only, at an event where the judge is judging classes other than Junior Showmanship.

Section 5. Safety.

Juniors with varying degrees of experience and dogs with great differences in size, temperament, and training need safe ring conditions. Judges must make every effort to ensure the safety of the Juniors and their dogs during competition. Judges should arrange or rearrange competitors in order of gaiting speed or size of dog to avoid crowding and instruct Juniors to leave adequate space between themselves and the Junior in front of or behind them. Moving two dogs together (side by side) is discouraged, as is any pattern which places any dog in close proximity to other dogs when lead control is at a minimum, e.g., on a loose lead, etc. In large classes judges should admit only as many Juniors into the ring as can be safely examined. Never hesitate to divide any class for any reason where the safety of the individuals or the dogs is involved. Likewise, do not hesitate to excuse from the ring any dog which is out of control, lame, or which is otherwise ineligible to compete. Any dog showing signs of menacing or threatening behavior should be excused immediately. Any dog that attacks any individual in the ring shall be disqualified in accordance with Chapter 11, Section 8A, of the Rules Applying to Dog Shows. In the case of a disqualification the judge must inform the Junior that the dog is not eligible to be exhibited again at any AKC event, and complete the necessary form for disqualifying a dog for attacking. Advise the Junior to speak with the AKC field representative about the reinstatement policy.

Section 6. Judging Routine.

The actual routine of judging is to be consistent with the procedures utilized when judging conformation. The number of Juniors, size of the ring, ring conditions, weather, and time of day will influence the actual procedures used. Judges will strive to evaluate competitors in an appropriate and consistent manner. It is essential that only the gaiting patterns and procedures used in regular dog show classes be used.

It is the responsibility of the judge to be aware of the appropriate presentation for all breeds, which is to include knowledge of which breeds are normally examined on a table. Upon request, the superintendent will provide the list of breeds entered in Junior Showmanship.

It is urged that the judge request each Junior to present their dog individually for examination, allowing the judge to observe the rapport between the Junior and the dog while being set up on either the ground or the table. Judges should ask the Junior to show the dog's bite, although with younger Juniors judges should use their discretion. The procedure for completing the examination of the dogs should closely resemble that of breed judging but need only be cursory, as the quality of the dog is not being evaluated. Judges should be consistent with every Junior, using the same gaiting patterns, the same procedural requests, and allowing each Junior approximately the same amount of time. Judges may revise the gaiting patterns when making final decisions. A judge should not confuse the ability of a Junior to take directions with the Junior's ability to handle his dog. Some freedom of expression and expertise should be allowed.

Judges should consider how their own movements in the ring might precipitate awkward and unusual handling results. For example, when examining the class as a whole in motion, the judge should be inside the circle; and when examining a class of standing or posed dogs the judge should not move from one side of the line to the other, creating unnecessary movements.

Judges should limit conversation with Juniors during competition to that which is absolutely necessary. However, judges should be prepared to answer Juniors' questions following judging and be able to provide positive comments and constructive criticism. UNDER NO CIRCUMSTANCES SHOULD QUESTIONS BE USED AS A MEANS

OF TESTING A JUNIOR'S KNOWLEDGE. A suggestion: if the Junior asks for comments following the judging, ask them to return with their dog, time permitting, and review their presentation.

Section 8. Judge's Examination and Evaluation.

The judge should examine and evaluate the class of Juniors in four basic areas: proper breed presentation, skill in the individual dog's presentation, knowledge of ring procedures, and appearance and conduct. The general rule in evaluating a handler's capabilities is ECONOMY OF MOTION. Handlers who use exaggerated motions and gestures in any phase of their presentation of the dog should be faulted. In essence, the judge should hardly be aware of the capable handler's presence while completing the dog's examination. In many respects a Junior Showmanship judge's principal consideration should be to find those Juniors who possess a "hand for dogs." Those handlers having this attribute neither over- nor under-handle their dogs. They present their dogs in a quiet, efficient manner. They are able to keep their dog's attention without dramatic or unnatural movements. They are able to gait their dogs in a collected trot, never distracting or interfering with the judge's vision of the dog.

Breed Presentation. While the judge must consider all areas important in evaluating the overall capabilities of Juniors, it is doubly important both that the Junior present his dog in the proper manner for the breed being handled and that the judge be cognizant of the proper presentation for that breed. It is imperative, therefore, that the judge have prior knowledge of the breeds which are to be presented and familiarity with the proper ways of handling those breeds. If the show superintendent or show secretary does not furnish a list of those breeds in the Judging Program, then the judge should request the list well in advance of the show date. In the individual presentation of the dog, the Junior should demonstrate the ability to handle the dog as it is handled in the breed ring, showing the dog to its best advantage in pose and in motion. During all phases of handling the Junior's concentration should be on the dog and not on the judge, but not to the extent that the Junior is unaware of what is taking place in the ring. Remember, you are judging the handler, but time should be spent looking at the dog to gain insight as to how well it is being handled.

- Is the dog responsive to the handler? Do dog and handler work as a team?
- Does the dog appear posed or interested at all times?
- Is the dog under control?
- Is the dog moved correctly to the best of its ability?
- Are the dog's main faults being minimized?

- Do both the dog and handler appear relaxed?
- Is the dog presented with an apparent minimum of effort?

Knowledge of Ring Procedure. The judge shall evaluate the ability of the Junior to follow directions, use space wisely, and execute the requested gaiting patterns. Juniors should appear "ring wise," be alert to the judging progression, and be prepared for changes in the judging routine.

Appearance and Conduct. The judge should be aware of the appearance of both the handler and the dog. The Junior should be suitably dressed for the occasion, wearing clothing that will not hinder or detract from the presentation of the dog. The dog should be groomed and trimmed in the manner associated with the breed for conformation. However, the judge should not evaluate either the dress of the handler or the grooming of the dog, but rather that an effort has been made. Excessive grooming of the dog in the ring to gain the judge's attention is inappropriate and should be faulted accordingly.

The judge shall evaluate the general conduct of Juniors in the ring. Juniors should appear prepared, confident, businesslike and attentive. They should be courteous to both the judge and their fellow exhibitors. Juniors are expected to handle their dogs without distracting the dogs of other competitors, and a Junior who crowds or disturbs other dogs should be faulted. A principle of Junior Showmanship is to afford the opportunity to learn the spirit of competition. Winning is important but is secondary to development of sportsmanship in competition. Judges who reward unsportsmanlike conduct or actions, regardless of a handler's other capabilities, compromise the very premise of Junior Showmanship.

Juniors should be alert to the needs of their dogs, realizing that the welfare of their dogs is important. Juniors are responsible for the control of their dogs at all times. However, Juniors who exhibit impatience or heavy-handedness with their dogs should be penalized.

Regulations for Junior Showmanship

Section 3. Standard for Judging.

Junior Showmanship shall be judged solely on the ability and skill of the Juniors in handling their dogs as in the breed ring. The show qualities of the dogs shall not be considered. Junior Handlers shall not be required to exchange dogs. The judge must excuse a handler and dog from the ring if, in his opinion, the handler cannot properly control the dog.

Section 4. Approval of Judges.

The criteria for eligibility to judge Junior Showmanship at an AKC All Breed event include experience in at least two of the following:
- Having been a Junior

- Being the Parent of a Junior
- Having been a Professional Handler
- Having taught handling classes
- Having judged Junior Showmanship at least three times at AKC All-Breed Sanctioned Matches
- Having attended a seminar on the judging of Junior Showmanship in the last 24 months.

Any Junior no longer eligible to compete in Junior Showmanship competition may apply for approval to judge Junior Showmanship.

Section 5. Classes and Divisions.

The regular Junior Showmanship Classes shall be:

(A) Novice. This class shall be for boys and girls who are at least 9 years old and under 18 years old on the day of the show and who at the time entries close have not won three (3) first place awards, with competition present, in a Novice Class at a licensed or member show.

(B) Open. This class shall be for boys and girls who are at least 9 years old and under 18 years old on the day of the show, and who have won three (3) first place awards in a Novice class in a licensed or member show, with competition present. The winner of a Novice class shall automatically become eligible, upon notice to the Open class ring steward, to enter and compete in the Open Class at the same show provided the win is the third (3rd) first place award with competition and further providing there are one or more Junior Handlers competing in the Open Class.

Junior Handlers who win a third Novice class with competition present after the closing of entries for a show may transfer their entry from the Novice class to the Open class provided that this transfer is made by the superintendent or show secretary at least one-half hour prior to the scheduled start of Junior Showmanship judging at the show.

No entry may be changed or cancelled unless notice of the change or cancellation is received in writing or by telegram by the superintendent or show secretary named in the premium list to receive entries, except that a correction may be made from one age division to another. This transfer must be made to the superintendent or show secretary at least one half-hour prior to the judging of any Junior Showmanship class at the show.

(C) Junior, Intermediate, and Senior classes. Either or both of these regular classes may be divided by age into Junior, Intermediate, and Senior classes, provided the division is specified in the premium list. A Junior class shall be for boys and girls who are at least 9 years old and under 12 years old on the day of the show. An Intermediate class shall be for boys and girls who are at least 12 years old and under 15 years old on the day of the show. A Senior class shall be for boys and girls who are at least 15 years old and under 18 years old on the day of the show.

Section 7. Eligibility of Dog.

Each dog entered in a regular Junior Showmanship class must be of a breed eligible to compete in conformation classes (including Miscellaneous classes) at the time of the event. The dog must be entered in one of the breed, obedience, or agility classes at the shows or must be entered for Junior Showmanship Only. An eligible dog other than the one entered may be substituted. Such substitution must be accompanied by an official AKC entry form. The junior must have the AKC number of the substitute dog. All such substitutions must be made at least one half hour prior to the judging of any Junior Showmanship classes at the show. Each dog must be owned by the Junior Handler or by the Junior Handler's father, mother, brother, sister, uncle, aunt, grandfather, or grandmother, including the corresponding step and half relations, or by a member of the Junior Handler's household. BITCHES IN SEASON ARE NOT ELIGIBLE. At a Specialty Show, each dog must be of the breed for which the show is held. A Junior is limited to one substitution at a dog show. If one of the owners of the dog is a judge, the dog may be entered in Junior Showmanship Only to be exhibited by the Junior at an event where the judge is judging classes other than Junior Showmanship.

Section 10. Closing of Entries.

Entries for regular Junior Showmanship classes shall close at the same time entries close for the show.

Section 15. Limited Junior Showmanship Classes

Limited Junior Showmanship classes shall be open only to Junior handlers who have qualified by reason of certain wins in Junior Showmanship competition as specified in the premium list within a specified period of about 12 months ending not more than 3 months prior to the date of the show; and may be further limited to Junior Handlers who reside within a specified geographical area or who have qualified at shows held within a specified geographical area.

Section 16. Exceptions for Limited Classes.

All of these regulations relating to regular Junior Showmanship classes shall also apply to Limited Junior Showmanship classes except that:

(A) The premium list or a separate announcement may specify a closing date or acceptance of entries in Limited Junior Showmanship classes later than the date for closing of entries in the show.

(B) The dogs handled in Limited Junior Showmanship must be eligible for entry in Dog Shows or Obedience Trials. They may, but need not, be entered in breed or obedience at the particular show. Any limitation or restriction on entries in a show shall not apply to dogs that are brought on the show premises only to be handled in Limited Junior Showmanship.

(C) The information on dogs to be handled in Limited Junior Showmanship that are not entered in the show, and the names of the Junior Handlers, must be given in the catalog.

(D) The age limits specified in Section 4 shall apply to the age of each Junior handler at the time of the last win required to qualify for the Limited Junior Showmanship class, rather than to the age on the date of the Limited Junior Showmanship competition.

(E) If the entries in Limited Junior Showmanship warrant, the club may specify, in the first or in a later announcement, that preliminary classes will be held at the show, from which the judge(s) will select a specified number of Juniors to compete for Best Junior Handler, and no placements will be made in the preliminary classes.

(F) If, after the close of entries for a Limited Junior Showmanship competition, it develops that for any reason a dog to be handled in the competition cannot be shown, the Junior handler may substitute another otherwise eligible dog, provided he supplies the superintendent or show secretary with the required identifying information on the dog prior to the start of judging of the class in which the Junior handler is to compete. (See Section 7 above.)

Appendix 2: Canadian Kennel Club Rules and Regulations

Reprinted by permission of the Canadian Kennel Club. These regulations are abridged to omit technicalities of importance only to judges or show-giving clubs.

PURPOSE

The purpose of Junior Handling is to introduce and encourage youth to participate in the sport of purebred dogs, and to provide them with meaningful competition where they can learn, practice, and hone their skills and knowledge of the various breeds. Above all, it is an opportunity to enjoy the camaraderie of competing with those of a similar age.

1 Interpretations

1.1 Definitions

For the purpose of these rules and regulations, the following interpretations shall apply:

"Board" means the Board of Directors of The Canadian Kennel Club

"CKC" means The Canadian Kennel Club

"Club" means The Canadian Kennel Club

"club" means a club or association officially recognized by The Canadian Kennel Club

"dog" means a purebred dog of either sex

"exhibitor" means the owner or handler who enters in a Junior Handling competition

"handler" means the person handling the dog in competition

"Head Office" means the office at which the business of The Canadian Kennel Club is carried out on a regular and ongoing basis

"Representative" means an individual appointee by the Board member from the respective zone to act as a liaison between clubs and participants

These rules shall be read with all applicable changes in gender so that the masculine shall include the feminine and vice versa, and the singular shall include the plural if applicable, and vice versa.

2.4.2 The CKC stresses the need to ensure that the fun element stays in all junior handling competitions and dog-related events.

3 General Rules and Regulations

3.4 Entries

3.4.1 Junior handlers shall have the opportunity to enter a junior handling competition by completing a preregistration form if available, or by completing the entry form at least one hour in advance of the scheduled judging on the day of the event. The entry form shall include the following information:

(a) Name of event-giving club and date of event.

(b) Name, address, and telephone number of the junior handler.

(c) Date of birth and signature of the junior handler.

(d) Class entered.

(e) Breed and catalogue number of the dog to be handled.

(f) Junior handler number, if available.

3.5 Eligibility of Dog

3.5.1 A junior handler may compete with any dog duly entered in the event, provided he has obtained the consent of the owner or agent to do so. The dog may be spayed or neutered provided that it is entered in the show or trial. The junior handler will wear the armband assigned to the dog for the regular event. Substitution of dogs will be allowed during the course of the competition.

3.5.2 Dogs being used in these competitions must be of the appropriate size and temperament to enable the junior handler to compete to the best of his ability. The Junior Kennel Club representative, his designate (or a show official if the former are not available), has the authority to monitor and remove a handler and dog from the ring if, in his opinion, it is necessary to prevent a situation which could potentially disrupt the competition.

3.5.3 A junior handler who uses a dog which is not entered in the show or trial will have his wins cancelled for that show or trial.

3.5.4 The use of bitches in season in junior competitions is at the discretion of the zone representative, excluding Pee Wees and Obedience. In the absence of the zone representative, the club shall have full discretionary power on the use of bitches in season.

4 Conformation

4.1 Conformation Class Structure

4.1.1 Classes in Junior Conformation Handling competition shall be divided by age as follows:

(a) Pee Wee Class

This class is for handlers 4 to 6 years of age as of December 31st of the competition year. This class is optional and noncompetitive. No placements are to be awarded; only participant ribbons, rosettes and token trophy may be presented.

(b) Junior Novice Class

This class is for handlers 7 years of age and up to and including 11 years of age as of December 31st of the competition year, who have not won six first places in the same class, with competition.

(c) Junior Open Class

This class is for handlers 7 years of age and up to and including 11 years of age as of December 31st of the competition year who have won six first places with competition. It is understood that once the handler has entered and competed in the Junior Open Class, he may not compete in the Junior Novice Class again.

(d) Senior Novice Class

This class is for handlers 12 years of age and up to but not including 18 years of age as of December 31st of the competition year who have not won six first places with competition in this class. Handlers from the Junior levels progress to this class.

(e) Senior Open Class

This class is for handlers 12 years of age and up to but not including 18 years of age as of December 31st of the competition year who have won six first places with competition in the Senior Novice Class, and for any handler who has progressed through the Junior Open level and feels that he has enough experience to compete at this level. This class is also for handlers who have received some type of monetary consideration for showing a dog at the Junior or Senior level.

4.1.2 Method of moving between classes shall be as follows:

(a) If a handler achieves six first place wins with competition, he must move to the Open class within his age group.

(b) Handlers can only move from the Pee Wee class or Junior class on December 31st of the same year of their birth date.

(c)   Points are to be carried forward from one level to the next.

4.4   Tabulation of Points

4.4.1   It is recommended that for all junior handling competitions, the Junior Kennel Club representative or tabulator record the allocated points.

Four placements will be made in each class:

First	Second	Third	Fourth
100	75	50	25

4.4.2   Points are to be tabulated from January 1 to December 31 of a calendar year.

4.5   End of Show

4.5.3   If a junior handler competes in a zone other than that of his residence, all points awarded to the handler will be forwarded to the representative or tabulator in his zone once the junior handler has completed the Out of Area form, signed by the judge or show official, and forwarded it to the zone representative. It is the responsibility of the junior handler to return this form to his representative within 30 days of the competition in order for the points for that competition to be counted. In this way it would be impossible for a junior to qualify in more than one zone.

5   Provincial/zone Competition Finals

5.1   Provincial/zone junior handling competitions shall be held once a year in order to select a Best Junior Handler for each of the CKC designated zones.

5.2   Junior handlers eligible for these competitions will be permitted to compete in only one of the competitions in any one year in the area where they are residing as of December 31st of the calendar year in which they establish their eligibility.

5.3   A maximum of the top four in each class will be eligible to compete at the zone finals. In case of a tie for any of the top four placements, all juniors eligible for those placements will be invited to compete in the finals.

5.6   The rules of the provincial/zone finals shall be the same as the rules for local competition with the following exceptions:

(a)   It shall be judged by a minimum of three judges. One of the judges will be responsible for ring procedures while the others shall act as observers. After consulting with each other the judges will select their winners. Score sheets must be used to determine the placements.

(b)   There will be four classes with a maximum of competitors in each class (except in the case of ties in any of the class placements).

(c) There will be two placements in each class, which shall be a Winner and Reserve Winner in each of the following classes:

Junior—Novice and Open

Senior—Novice and Open

5.7 The winner in each class at the zone finals will compete for top zone finalist.

5.8 The handler who places second in the class from which the best overall winner is chosen together with the winners of the other three classes shall be eligible to compete for runner-up.

5.9 A rosette and trophy may be provided for the winner and runner-up. Other prizes and ribbons may be offered to the winners or all handlers.

5.10 A rosette and trophy may also be provided for the junior handler accumulating the most points in junior handling competitions at championship shows during the previous year. This award will be designated highest aggregate provincial junior handling competition. The trophy offered may be a perpetual trophy, or any other type at the discretion of the zone representative.

6 National Competition—Conformation

6.1 The National Competition (conformation) is to be held before December 31st of the year following establishment of eligibility.

6.2 The winner of each provincial/zone competition will be invited to compete.

6.3 The winner of this competition will be declared the Top Canadian Junior Handler. A reserve winner will also be chosen.

6.4 First to fourth placements will be chosen. The first place winner of this competition will be declared Top Canadian Junior Handler, the second place winner will be declared the reserve winner.

6.6 At the national competition, classes will not be divided.

6.7 The rules of judging will be identical to those used in zone final competitions, with the following exceptions:

(a) The competition will be judged by five judges; one of the five will be responsible for ring procedures while the other four will score the handlers.

(b) Depending on the size and manageability of the dogs involved, the judge may request the handlers competing at this level to exchange dogs in the ring in order to verify the extent of the handler's skill and knowledge.

Appendix A: Judging Guidelines—Conformation

1.1　The overall impression is most important. The judge shall look for a junior handler appropriately dressed who presents his dog in a manner which will display its particular breed characteristics to its advantage. Conformation of the dog is not to be considered in the assessment of the handler's ability. Therefore, the judge should be aware of the way particular breeds are handled.

(a)　The handler must use the proper breed stance; e.g., German shepherd with a leg stretch, various sporting breeds with head up and tail out, collies free baited with little stacking, bloodhounds with lots of wrinkle piled up, etc. All breeds should be shown in a suitable manner appropriate for the time and reflecting current fashions.

(b)　Handlers must have acceptable show attire and be well groomed. Clothing and hairstyles that interfere with the showing of the dog to be penalized. In particular, shoes should have nonslip soles and be of a size and style that does not endanger the dog or handler. All exhibitors should appear to be neat and clean. Attention should be paid to colours and patterns that do not detract from the dog, e.g., any white clothes with a white dog. Clothing should not restrict movement and hemlines on girls should be appropriate for age and breed shown.

(c)　Conformation of the dog is not important but handlers should try to minimize faults and display virtues without excessive or distractive movements. Dogs with obvious faults such as crooked fronts or cowhocks should have those faults recognized and corrected by the handler as much as possible with handling techniques.

1.2　The judge should give credit to junior handlers who display good sportsmanship.

(a)　The handlers should give the impression of polite compliance to a judge's request in both facial features and body language without exaggeration.

(b)　The handlers demonstrate their courteousness towards each other by not crowding in the standing or gaiting situation. In large classes judges can split the class to provide adequate ring space.

(c)　The lead handler inquires of the next in line if the handler is ready and should wait for the others to organize their dogs before leading the group in a go around. If asked to move to a different place in line they must give the other exhibitors a chance to make room.

1.3　The handler and the dog should function as part of a team, unobtrusive but efficient. The handler should encourage his dog and under no circumstances should the handler forcibly discipline his dog in the ring. Should this occur, the handler will receive a substantial deduction of points.

1.4   The judge should look for that elusive "extra" in the handler's showmanship, the ability to display that feeling of pride in the dog and to exhibit his dog with flair and rapport.

(a)   The handler should be aware of the dog's quality and let the judge know that they are working to display these strengths. A dog that comes into a perfect free stance for instance should be occasion for the handler to give the judge an indication by a look or body language that they are pleased. The handler is not just a technician, but is an artist creating a picture with the dog's virtues. There should be recognition by the handler when that picture is close to what we consider to be beautiful. Excessive attention to the judge is a detriment and not a positive; e.g., too much smiling, inattention to the dog while gaiting by focusing on the judge.

1.5   The judge should give credit to the handler who has to deal with a difficult dog and handles the problem in a competent manner. Sometimes a handler who is exhibiting a highly trained dog appears to be very proficient when in reality the dog is handling itself.

(a)   Handlers who have worked hard to train a dog might give the impression of having an easy dog. Most dogs have a bad day from time to time and the handler's ability to deal with it is a measure of competency.

1.6   Outwardly shy or aggressive dogs should not be shown by junior handlers. See Section 3.5.2.

(a)   Dogs being used in these competitions must be of the appropriate size and temperament to enable the junior handler to compete to the best of his ability. The Junior Kennel Club representative or his designate has the authority to monitor and remove a handler and his dog from the ring if, in his opinion, it is necessary to prevent a situation which could potentially disrupt the competition.

(b)   The safety of the dogs and handlers must be of primary importance.

(c)   In the opinion of the judge, if a dog appears to be too difficult for the handler to control and the safety of the handler, the other handlers, or dogs is in question, the judge should do what is necessary to isolate the dog in the ring to ensure safety or in extreme cases to excuse the team. Chemistry between dogs and the size must be taken into account. Dogs for Pee Wee handlers should be 18 inches or less at the withers unless it is a breed renowned for its excessively mild temperament. If in doubt, err on the side of caution and delay the start of that class until a suitable replacement dog can be found.

1.7   Junior competitions are to promote quality handling and sportsmanship and the judge should never lose sight of this.

1.8 Junior handlers are reminded that they are not to engage in unnecessary conversation with other handlers or the judge.

1.9 A handler and his dog are not to interfere with another handler and his dog.

Appendix B: Ring Procedure—Conformation

1.1 The judge may use any examination pattern normally used in the conformation ring. The same pattern must be followed for each junior when the dogs are moved individually.

Common Patterns

The handlers come in as called by the ring steward and will be judged from the moment that they enter the ring. They stack dogs where the judge gets a first view. The judge may rearrange the dogs and they should be moved together. Each team gets an individual examination. They demonstrate an individual movement pattern and the free stack. In the more advanced classes the judge may add group stacks towards the front and rear, side by side down and backs used infrequently and exchanging of dogs at the Senior Open level. When exchanging of dogs is used, the ring steward and an assistant or the judge shall hold the dogs to facilitate an uneventful transfer. The handler should inquire as to the dog's name and any special instructions.

A grooming tool is permissible based on the breed shown; excessive tools and their use should be penalized.

1.2 The judge should inspect each dog individually, as this will indicate to the judge if the handler knows how to show the dog at close quarters. For example: each junior should have to show the bite and expression of the dog to the judge's satisfaction; feet can be placed incorrectly to see if the handler corrects this, etc.

Watch for the following actions by the handler. The junior poses the dog to present the side picture. The handler shows expression of the dog as the judge moves to the front of the dog. The judge approaches and the junior shows the bite in the manner normally used in the breed, e.g., full dentition for Dobes, tongue colour in Chows. As the judge goes over the front, the handler glances to check rear position has not shifted. The judge examines rear and the handler checks the front for movement. Junior checks for any movement as the judge moves to the side to get final picture, junior settles dog and poses it for the final look. Tabled breeds follow the above pattern and must be presented on a table if required at the breed level with the exception of the Pee Wee class, which is never examined on the table for the safety of the dog.

1.3 The dog should be moved with smoothness, grace, and at the correct speed for the breed.

1.4 The dog must be between the handler and the judge at all times, thus giving the judge ample opportunity to observe how the handler presents the dog.

1.5 The lead should be in the hand nearest the dog at all times. The lead must be folded up without any end trailing and not wrapped around the fingers while gaiting. Some handlers showing larger dogs have the lead looped around one finger for control purposes. In some breeds such as German shepherds, it is customary to use longer leads held in folds. Any difference in style should reflect the custom in various breed rings and should be honored in junior rings just as different posing styles are. The dog should always be under control and the overall look should be pleasing.

1.6 As a handler comes out to move his dog individually he should present the dog to the judge, allowing the dog to pose naturally. A courtesy turn is highly desirable. After gaiting, the handler should again allow the dog to pose naturally while baiting the dog before the judge.

1.7 When the handlers are moved individually, a pattern which requires a lead change from hand to hand such as a "crossover" is desired.

The dog should be moved with smoothness, grace, and at the correct speed for the breed. Judges should take into account that at certain stages of physical development the handler may appear awkward and should not be penalized. When handlers are gaited in the side-by-side down and back (only at Senior Open level and infrequently) the faster dog should be adjusted to the speed of the smaller dog and the handlers should ensure verbally and visually that they are both ready before proceeding.

Common patterns that may be used are as follows:
- Up and Back
- Triangle
- "L"
- Reverse Triangle
- Reverse "L"
- "T"

The handler must switch smoothly whenever the judge moves around the dog to ensure that the judge's view of the dog is not blocked in the free stack at the end of the pattern. Excessive movement around or over the dog is not required to assess the handler's ability. Most handlers perform a courtesy turn to present the dog to the judge before individually gaiting. All instructions as to what the desired pattern is should be given the whole line and given as many times as needed to make it possible for all handlers to hear them from the judge. Handlers can ask for instructions to be repeated in a polite manner.

A junior handler should be given appropriate time to get a free stack from the dog at the end of the individual gaiting.

1.8   It is highly desirable that the judge asks questions of the handlers, relating to commonly known information regarding the breed shown, anatomy, or common show terms. For consistency and to fairly assess the handler's ability, each handler is to be asked identical questions. These questions should not be used to break a tie.

When asking questions, the judge should keep in mind the age level and apparent skill level of the competitors. Competitors should not see or hear the answers of the others.

1.9   At local competitions the exchange of dogs is not permitted except at the Senior Open level and then only at the discretion of the judge.

1.10   At zone finals, the exchange of dogs may be permitted at the discretion of the judge.

1.11   Judges and junior handlers should be mindful at all times that while excellence of accomplishment is to be sought, the enjoyment and experience of participation is more important than winning. Special attention should be given to the obvious rapport of the handler with the dog. Good sportsmanship should always be encouraged, and you should observe and encourage the handlers in congratulating the winners. Winners should also be encouraged to accept their placements with grace and humility. Judges make themselves available to exhibitors for pictures as soon after competition as feasible.

Judges should also encourage improvement in the juniors by offering constructive criticism. Judges must be sensitive to the feelings of the youngsters and realize that although some handlers will be especially successful in the junior handling competitions and the others may not be, this success is not indicative of a handler's future potential in the fancy. Some who have gone on to be very valuable in the dog fancy for a lifetime were spectacularly unsuccessful as Junior handlers. Others that have shown in the Junior Handling ring dropped out as they grew older because they were more interested in the Junior level and when it ended for them, they moved on to other interests. There is nothing wrong with that, but judges should bear in mind that each contact with junior handlers could foster or destroy interest. If time permits, an oral critique of all the class benefits the handlers.

Appendix C: Suggested Questions for Junior Handlers—Conformation

The answers given at this level will demonstrate the knowledge of the handlers. Note that the following questions are suggestions only. At the discretion of the judge, other questions may be asked that are appropriate for the level of competition. In order to avoid any misunderstanding, all questions must be phrased clearly and completely.

General Questions

- What is the breed of your dog?
- What do you call the colour of your dog?
- What group does your dog belong to?
- What is the purpose of a dog show?
- What was your dog's breed used for?

When asking anatomy questions, they should be such that it is not necessary to point to a specific part of the dog thus providing a clue of the answer to the other handlers.

Where/what is the:
- Bite
- Wither
- Elbow
- Muzzle
- Stifle
- Occiput
- Metacarpus
- Croup
- Loin
- Feathering

Senior Questions

- What is the breed's purpose?
- What are the breed's disqualifying faults?
- Name the quality of your dog you want the judge to see.

When asking anatomy questions, it is not necessary point to a specific part of the dog thus providing a clue to the answer.

Where/what is the:
- Pastern
- Loin
- Sternum
- Flew
- Flank
- Ischium
- Upper Arm
- Forechest
- Brisket
- Stifle
- Croup
- Stop

My Junior Handling Record

Date _____ Show _____ Location _____

Class _____ Place _____ Dog _____

Judge _____

Special Happenings _____

_____

_____

Comments about Judge _____

_____

Comments by Judge _____

_____

_____

- -

Date _____ Show _____ Location _____

Class _____ Place _____ Dog _____

Judge _____

Special Happenings _____

_____

_____

Comments about Judge _____

_____

Comments by Judge _____

_____

_____

- -

Date _____ Show _____ Location _____

Class _____ Place _____ Dog _____

Judge _____

Special Happenings _____

_____

_____

Comments about Judge _____

_____

Comments by Judge _____

_____

_____

My Junior Handling Record

Date _____ Show _____ Location _____

Class _____ Place _____ Dog _____

Judge _____

Special Happenings _____

_____

_____

Comments about Judge _____

_____

Comments by Judge _____

_____

_____

- -

Date _____ Show _____ Location _____

Class _____ Place _____ Dog _____

Judge _____

Special Happenings _____

_____

_____

Comments about Judge _____

_____

Comments by Judge _____

_____

_____

- -

Date _____ Show _____ Location _____

Class _____ Place _____ Dog _____

Judge _____

Special Happenings _____

_____

_____

Comments about Judge _____

_____

Comments by Judge _____

_____

_____

My Junior Handling Record

Date _____ Show _____ Location _____
Class _____ Place _____ Dog _____
Judge _____
Special Happenings _____
_____
_____

Comments about Judge _____
_____

Comments by Judge _____
_____
_____

- -

Date _____ Show _____ Location _____
Class _____ Place _____ Dog _____
Judge _____
Special Happenings _____
_____
_____

Comments about Judge _____
_____

Comments by Judge _____
_____
_____

- -

Date _____ Show _____ Location _____
Class _____ Place _____ Dog _____
Judge _____
Special Happenings _____
_____
_____

Comments about Judge _____
_____

Comments by Judge _____
_____
_____

Index